The Power to Learn
stories of success in the education of Asian and other bilingual pupils

The Power to Learn
stories of success in the education of Asian and other bilingual pupils

Terry Wrigley

Trentham Books

Stoke on Trent, UK and Sterling, USA

Trentham Books Limited

Westview House	22883 Quicksilver Drive
734 London Road	Sterling
Oakhill	VA 20166-2012
Stoke on Trent	USA
Staffordshire	
England ST4 5NP	

First published 2000, reprinted 2002

British Library Cataloguing-in-Publication Data
A catalogue record for this book is available from the British Library

1 85856 210 4 (paperback)

Designed and typeset by Trentham Print Design Ltd., Chester and printed in Great Britain by Biddles Ltd., Guildford.

Contents

Introduction

Improving schools? Raising achievement for all? Ten years ago, you had to be a very bold individual to believe this might be possible.

In many a school, the low achievement of Asian pupils was seen as sad but inevitable. 'If only we could persuade these parents to give up their false hopes of their sons becoming doctors or lawyers? They have such ridiculous expectations!' (The daughters, of course, were even further out of the frame.)

It has been a real pleasure and privilege to put together a book about schools which have turned the dream into reality. What a good thing that some teachers had the same 'ridiculous expectations' as the Asian community. Despite the gloomy educational politics of the time, these teachers clung to unfashionable ideologies of multiculturalism and antiracism to fight for the children's right to success.

Now, of course, it is no longer strange to believe in raising achievement; it has become mandatory. If some schools can do it, why not all? Leading politicians would prefer to ignore the uncomfortable fact that while schools do make a difference, a vital difference to their pupils' futures, *even teachers' most heroic efforts cannot wipe out the effects of urban poverty*. The drive for schools to improve, to the pupils' great benefit, must not be allowed to make teachers scapegoats for the social problems of our economic and political system. This would be just as damaging as complacency at low achievement.

A widespread but inadequate version of school improvement theory, supposedly derived from the most successful schools, is being promoted by some politicians, government officials and newspaper editors. At its worst, it amounts to the belief that if only teachers would show more willing, flick a mental switch to 'high expectations' and *drive* themselves and their pupils to work harder, exam results would soar. The management model being promoted is one of 'strings the Head should pull' to make the puppet dance. No thought is given to what lies at the end of the string. Of course, they'll need a *vision*, though it's not entirely clear what it is they need to *see*. Partnership with parents, and the school ethos, are understood, in a reductionist form, as *making sure the homework gets done and tightening up on behaviour*.

My many visits to schools which are achieving success for disadvantaged pupils, as a school inspector and then a university researcher, have left me in no doubt that school improvement is a matter of *empowerment*, not control. Hence the title of this book: *The Power to Learn*. All the monitoring and data collection and target setting are only effective to the extent that they support a philosophy and practice of empowerment, for pupils, staff and parents.

I have been keen to interpret achievement in the broadest sense – not only literacy and numeracy scores, or even the number of higher grade GCSEs, but achievement across the full spectrum of the school curriculum and beyond, as personal and social and cultural and political development. The measurable attainment is important, indeed vital, for the future of the individual pupil but it is not enough:

> We need young people who are skilled tabla players and computer users, who enjoy Asian films and Western books, who are able to lead themselves and their communities forward through change and storm and a calm sea, who are socially aware and morally committed and no one's fool. We need a very wide definition of achievement. (Wrigley, 1997, p25)

Visiting one school after another, from Glasgow to London, my hypotheses were repeatedly confirmed:

• In *school development*, visions have to be shared and formed collectively. Social commitment and reflective professional partnership are of greater significance than mere pressure from the top downwards.

- The *curriculum* is not something fixed and waiting to be 'delivered'; instead teachers need to be assertive and creative enough to develop a curriculum which meets the learners' needs.

- *Teaching and learning* are the main force in raising achievement. Bilingual pupils in particular need activities which promote their cognitive, linguistic and social development.

- *Motivation* through extrinsic rewards can only do so much, since successful learning depends ultimately on the learner believing in its value, and on a culture in which each pupil's achievement leads to public esteem from peers and parents.

- *School ethos* is about more than ensuring discipline and diligence. It depends on the development of the school as a *community within a community*, on the quality and equality of internal and external *relationships* and of the *values* they express.

Part A of the book deals with these issues at a more theoretical level, and develops some material already published elsewhere (Wrigley, 1997 and 2000). Part B consists of ten case studies of schools. Part C is a brief conclusion, with proposals for continued development.

To avoid repetitious footnotes, an appendix provides a short guide to the education systems of England and Scotland, and to terminology used in this book. I hope this is of value to readers who are not entirely familiar with these education systems.

* * *

I would like to thank the staff and headteachers for allowing me into their schools and classrooms, extending great hospitality and finding time to engage with me in discussion in between all their other tasks. They are the real authors of this book, through their work and thought over many years. I have tried to acknowledge the contribution of the teachers whose lessons I saw – a great privilege – and of the people who spoke to me at length. I apologise to those whose names I have inadvertently omitted, and to all the other fine staff in these schools who, for reasons of time and space, are not featured. Nor should my selection of schools be taken to imply that there aren't many others just as good.

I would also like to thank Gillian Klein of Trentham Books for first prompting me to write, and for her patience and confidence through many delays; the University of Edinburgh for allowing me the time and funding for the school research, and my colleagues for engaging in discussion; and my family, for their support and encouragement.

PART A – THE ISSUES

What counts as achievement for bilingual pupils?

The ability to understand, communicate and think in two or more languages is in itself a great achievement. To many teachers working in multi-ethnic schools, this will seem obvious, and yet it is just one of the many achievements which go unrecorded.

So too is pupils' intercultural awareness and confidence, their ability to move between different social structures and value systems, to empathise and contribute. Nor is everything sweetness and light: there is also the ability to challenge, to form their own judgements. They need to know when to appreciate tradition and when to lift its repressive weight off their shoulders. They need to tackle poverty and racist injustice. These achievements are not measured in assessment data and league tables but they are of crucial importance for the individuals, for our communities, and for humanity.

This is not to suggest that exam results don't matter. They matter even more if you're black, working class, or both, because they are an irrefutable marker of what you've achieved. More privileged youngsters may still be able to slide into positions, using their school reputation, family influence and elegant breeding as entry tickets, but for ethnic minority students, certificates of qualification have always been the first proof. Not that they are enough, in a society run through with subtle racism.

Michael Fullan, I believe, coined the slogan, 'We should measure what we value, not value what we measure.' Of course, we also need to value what we cannot possibly measure – a salutary reminder, given current obsessions with testing and comparative data. Again, this is not to suggest that data analysis, involving value added and comparisons between schools, is worthless, but we do need to take care.

In the early nineties, the Thatcher government ordered the publication of school assessment data, which local and national newspapers were delighted to print as 'league tables'. There arose the naïve belief that if 95 per cent of pupils at King Midas Grammar School could achieve 5 A*-C grades but far fewer did so at Coketown Comprehensive, then the Coketown teachers must be to blame or the school must be a concrete jungle. This accelerated 'white flight', as many parents chose to move house or bus their children to suburban schools.

Although the reliance on raw data is now tempered by a 'benchmarking' system which attempts to compare 'similar' schools, the measures are crude and only take into account the proportion of pupils known to be entitled to free meals. Meanwhile, the newspapers continue to rely on the raw data.

At the same time, we must recognise that there are vast differences between schools which cannot be explained by circumstances. Some of the schools featured in this book have achieved dramatic improvements in exam success while intakes and levels of disadvantage have remained constant. If 30 per cent of pupils in School A achieve five or more A*-C grades at GCSE compared with 5 per cent at School B, this could make an enormous difference to the futures of a quarter of the pupils. And if 25 per cent of pupils at School B leave with no GCSEs at all, whereas all pupils at School A gain some, then another quarter may have their futures blighted.

How to steer between Scylla and Charybdis? To ignore the impact of social circumstances and selection (open or covert) and set impossible targets is the high road to demoralisation. At the other extreme, the sociological determinism which insists that different levels of attainment in schools are entirely the products of social circumstances is as harmful as genetic determinism – it simply reinforces disadvantage and reproduces poverty.

We need to take particular care when using data to evaluate the quality of education in schools with large proportions of bilingual pupils. Language development takes time. In some areas, particularly the former textile manufacturing towns of Lancashire and West Yorkshire, Asian children spend their early years in a discrete community where little English is spoken. The school's first task is to develop the spoken language of everyday transactions and association. Even when children arrive at school with this skill, it may take many years before they become fluent writers of academic English. This, of course, sits on top of the wider issue (affecting bilingual and monolingual children alike) of the different levels of scientific and social discourse to which pupils are accustomed at home, with its effect on cognitive and linguistic development and on social integration into the school culture.

To ignore these factors and make premature comparisons is a grave error. The 'free school meal' indicator is only a starting point. Over-anxiety about test results can lead to a drive to teach 'literacy' in ways that undermine its stated goal, and it denies bilingual pupils the rich linguistic and experiential foundation upon which their future educational success depends.

* * *

In selecting the ten schools for this book, I have taken into account a range of factors but have always looked towards achievement in the broadest sense. In almost all cases, the published assessment data provides clear evidence of high achievement or dramatic improvement. This turned out to be more difficult in the Scottish schools, where the national assessment database is less developed.

At the same time, among the criteria for including any school, I have looked for indicators of educational breadth, of achievement and progress in many different dimensions.

The schools selected are at different stages in their development. Their current headteachers have been in post for between one and fifteen years. They have taken different paths, responding to their specific communities, learning from official wisdom on school improvement, drawing from the best aspects of the latest government initiatives, adapting official requirements of national curricula and literacy hours to meet their pupils' needs in divergent ways, and thus developing unique strengths. Achievement, of necessity, means something different in each of these schools.

It follows that they are offered here not as a simple blueprint, a pattern for others to copy. Rather, the hope is that other schools will learn from what has been achieved by these pupils, and will build upon their own existing strengths in order to achieve new and diverse forms of success in their turn.

Whole-school factors
supporting success

Many attempts have been made over the past decade to list the factors promoting school improvement. It has become the convention to list ten or twelve 'characteristics', which then take on the status of a set of rules for heads to follow.

One problem with this approach is that issues become over-simplified. In the attempt to formulate one-liners and bullet-points, the complexity of practice is distilled into a few words which others then read from a quite different perspective. One interesting example concerns the quality of headship. The descriptor 'strong positive leadership' (National Commission on Education, 1996, p366) or, more crudely, 'a strong headteacher', is capable of multiple inter-pretation. Clearly, a weak headteacher can seriously damage the health of your school, but on the other hand, many of us would not share OFSTED Chief Inspector's notion of 'strong'. The quality of leadership demonstrated by each of the headteachers featured in this book is clearly a major contributor to their school's success, yet their style and patterns differ. Equally important is the quality of the staff, the culture of collaboration and reflectiveness among the teachers, the leadership and initiative of key staff such as heads of department, and often including the EAL specialists. In fact, the two aspects can-not rightly be separated: the quality of leadership by the headteacher is outstanding because of their personal qualities and because of the collegial strength. It is a dialectic. If 'strong' means imaginative and courageous and sensitive and socially committed, then 'strong leadership' is fine, but these are frequently not the connotations that first spring to mind.

Similarly, it is all too easy to reduce the quality of relationships to good discipline, or reduce parental cooperation to simply ensuring that pupils attend and that homework gets done. 'Well developed procedures for assessing how pupils are progressing' (National Commission on Education, 1996, p366) implies that the assessment will itself make a difference, however it is used and disregarding the climate within which pupils are told their results. 'Participation by pupils in the life of the school' has been reduced to the issue of whether there are school prefects! (p183) There is a common thread in this reductionism: it is an authoritarian simplification, based on a particular notion of schooling and a view of education which is, to say the least, problematic.

In the Introduction, I pointed to a number of areas for exploration:

- a broad understanding of achievement – academic, cultural, social

- the collegiality of school development processes

- a meaningful curriculum

- active learning involving cognitive, linguistic and social development

- an ethos of achievement

- relationships within the school and with the wider community.

The reader will find that these run throughout the stories that follow. It is the practice of the schools, which I have often told in narrative form so as to illustrate the prevailing philosophy, which will prevent these bullet-points being misinterpreted.

* * *

The success factors for bilingual pupils and multiethnic schools show many similarities to the practices of successful and improving schools in more monocultural urban environments. A good deal of mutual learning can take place when good practice is shared, but it has to be rethought and shaped to fit different circumstances.

In a mainly white school (Heywood Community School, Rochdale) I once visited, on a very deprived housing estate, the head and deputies didn't need an *open-door policy*. They didn't even have a door! They had taken the dramatic step of moving from their offices to a former classroom, from which the head physically removed the door. Pupils and staff no longer needed to talk their way past the secretary to see the Head. Similarly, bringing management closer to Asian parents is a crucial issue, in light of their often negative experience of officialdom, both in England and in the Sub-continent. Translating letters home is only part of the picture. Having teachers and classroom assistants from the local community on the staff and on the Senior Management Team can be an enormous asset.

I used to be sceptical about 'PR' but have come to understand how important it is to foster a warm respect for the school. Parents who have suffered disappointments in their own education and who are living in areas of poor housing or unemployment, can easily project their own low self-esteem onto the school – 'a school situated here can't be much good.' It is important to counter this attitude in every way possible, through drama or musical events, displays or by highlighting the school's achievements in the local paper. How often do we see pupils' work displayed in public places such as the community centre or the mosque?

Raising expectations is not just a matter of changing teachers' minds, or of putting more pressure on pupils to aim higher. It involves a complex set of cultural practices. In schools where low achievement is endemic, a visible breakthrough needs to be made, and everybody has to know about it. Asian parents are proud to know their children are doing well.

Creating an achievement culture may mean establishing a strong counter-culture to the street environment, especially for boys. They need to feel a real thrill about their school work, gaining high self-esteem from what they produce there. It is easy to underestimate how peer pressure can deter boys in particular from achieving in school, unless the school can sweep them along in a current that makes them all glad to achieve. Our tradition of schooling is highly individual. Too often, the only outcome from a pupil's work is a piece of writing, for the teacher to correct but for no one in particular to read for any real purpose. For older pupils the currency of extrinsic rewards such as merit certificates eventually becomes devalued, simply reinforcing a school culture where the tasks always seem miles from reality and never valid in themselves. To create an achievement culture, work of all kinds has to be collectively valued

– displayed, read aloud, acted out, sat on, eaten, printed, performed, enjoyed. (Wrigley, 1997 p22)

This is one of many reasons why *the arts* are so important. I once saw a class of 14-year-olds rehearsing a dance – without a 'teacher' but encouraged and guided by their school cleaner. They were rehearsing for the school assembly and it was all part of the process of *raising self-esteem*, convincing the children they were special. Active participation in the expressive and performing arts is integral to personal development and crucial in any school which seeks to boost achievement. It is more difficult when artistic involvement is condemned as either 'lower caste' or 'un-Islamic', but many of the schools featured in this book have overcome such difficulties, winning the parents over through their pride in the work displayed, combined with a measure of diplomacy. Defensiveness doesn't help, and teachers can derive confidence from acquiring knowledge of the vibrant cultural traditions of South Asians and the Muslim world.

The arts are also important as a site where *identities and cultures* are negotiated and a symbolic stance is taken against oppression. This links the arts with other parts of the curriculum where meanings are made and resisted, with language and media studies, with religious education and history, and so on. Asian and other bilingual pupils spend their lives moving between cultures and social structures. One of the greatest surprises of the research for this book was discovering such diverse practices developed to support this intercultural movement, to give it coherence and reflect on its meanings and values.

Three years ago, in that same Rochdale school, I was thrilled to hear some teachers describing their pupils as 'First Generation Academics'. This is such a powerful phrase because it turns on its head so neatly the old fatalism which says 'these pupils can't succeed because their parents didn't', or 'they've inherited low IQ', or are 'linguistically deprived'. This strand of determinism has led from the blunt Victorian pragmatism of 'Don't educate the working class above their station' to unproven assertions about a working class 'language deficit', into lingering expectations that children whose mums don't speak English are bound to fail.

'First Generation Academics' is a powerful phrase also because it demands that we think through without romanticism the relationship between school and community. The idea of establishing a culture of achievement within the school that must oppose the macho street culture has a degree of truth, but schools also need to be open to their environments. They need to be 'multicultural', but not in some tokenistic or idealised way. A deeper understanding of the tensions and contradictions of real lives is the basis for opening new doors for their pupils. Perhaps we need to think ahead more for parents, to take on that role when it comes to choosing options. We have to help pupils and parents to think futures – careers, lifestyles, opportunities they may know little about. Target-setting interviews, mentors, visits to universities, a wider work experience can all help fill the gap. We need not so much a 'Take Your Daughter to Work Day' as a 'Take Someone Else's'. This is not to disparage parents – we value their involvement and need them on board. Asian parents have pushed hard for their children to succeed in education. Some schools are beginning to focus their attention on older brothers and sisters, who are often major partners in their siblings' education. The link between pastoral and academic guidance is proving to be key to raising achievement in all schools, and has particular relevance to Asian and other bilingual pupils.

Finally, school development and staff development need to be approached with great thoroughness. School development is about more than just a neatly written plan. It involves a process of co-operative reflection, a critical look at the evidence, and development of an educational philosophy. *Commitment cannot be won lightly.* Similarly, for staff development to have a real impact on what happens in the classroom, it must be grounded in experience, inspired by a principled understanding, and fully supported until new practices become second nature. While recognising the value of top-down monitoring, the advances described in this book derive more from trusting partnership and cooperation between teachers. Peer-observation, within and between schools, is a crucial element of staff development. Partnerships established between EAL specialists and mainstream teachers have played a vital role in giving students the power to learn.

Teaching and learning

One of the most remarkable features of the vast literature on school improvement is its virtual silence on teaching and learning. This is in sharp contrast to the noise of the popular press, where attacks on 'progressive teaching' remain popular. England's Chief Inspector, Chris Woodhead, based on who knows what evidence, is also a keen supporter of 'traditional methods', though in Scotland the official line is for 'interactive expository teaching', whatever that might be. Leading politicians in the present government also seem intent on fighting a war against 'progressivism', as if a return to 'chalk and talk' and dictated notes were the answer, although this seems curiously at odds with a determination to forge ahead with Information and Communication Technology.

Having said this, I remain unsure of the value of fighting on this territory for quality teaching and learning. My belief is that didactic Punch beating up child-centred Judy, the Traditional versus Progressive match in endless action replays, does not move us forward because neither is a useful model of effective teaching and learning.

In his novel *Hard Times*, Dickens (1854) caricatured the 'didactic' method as teachers pouring facts and more facts into empty vessels. The didactic model overplays the teacher's role and denies the learner's, whilst limiting what transfers between them to bits of data. The 'progressive' or 'discovery' model of teaching and learning, in its purest form, centralises the pupil, reducing the teacher's role to creating an environment in which learning more or less spontaneously occurs. To simplify a rich tradition from Rousseau to Plowden, its central metaphor is that of nurturing a young plant – again, a reduction of the dynamic relationship between teachers and learners.

In practice, the most effective pedagogy values both *teachers and learners*. It is based upon *experience* and *intervention* and a *language-rich interaction* between both partners. It is hard to find a single pedagogical theory which articulates this fully, but some partial theories point in the same direction – towards skilful intervention based on valuing the learner's existing knowledge and generating a dynamic process of learning. Three sources come to mind.

Firstly Vygotsky (1962 and 1978), the revolutionary who was so impatient with Piaget's biological theory of development, whereby the teacher waits for the next stage of growth. For Vygotsky, intellectual development wasn't tied to age and stages of maturation but depended upon teachers skilfully assessing how their pupils were thinking, in order to lead them over the *threshold* onto a new level. The teacher is crucial because s/he helps the learners to do today with support what they will be able to do independently tomorrow. Vygotsky's 'psychology' starts in public, with language rather than with silent thought. Assessment is dynamic, looking to future as well as past, locating the 'zone of proximal development', identifying the threshold that the learner is approaching.

Secondly, the late Rosalind Driver (1983) of Leeds University, and the Children's Science project internationally. Extending the meaning of *Constructivism*, these researchers have explored the importance of bringing out into the open what the learners already know, their pre-existing models of reality, in order to move them to a new and more theoretical level. Far from being empty vessels, children have constructs of how the world works, based on their experience, their culture and their language. For example, learning about the conservation of matter is constantly undermined by the common-sense idea that things *burn away*, burn almost to nothing, a model which is reinforced by experience and language. Ignoring these everyday notions is no use; you need to bring them out into the open in order to combat them, or they will remain in the learner's mind alongside the scientific theory – a source of constant confusion. Thus *language* and *experience* and *skilled intervention* are again seen as crucial at the threshold of new learning.

The problem of holding two different theories, a common-sense one linked to everyday reality and the home culture, and an academic one lasting only during school hours and perhaps as far as the exam, could be even more intense for bilingual ethnic minority pupils. Although researchers have concluded that there is little difference in the pre-scientific theories held by pupils from different cultural backgrounds, the evidence is still limited and often derived from pupils who are already strongly accultured into Western learning. These two issues are worth exploring.

The new Constructivism has relevance far beyond science. I heard an interesting example of children in Ipswich, a coastal town far from any river source, who, when studying the water cycle, revealed their preconception that the water in rivers is pushed into them from the sea. We can usefully apply the pedagogical theories of Children's Science to many other domains: to history, to literature, to teaching about sexism and racism.

It follows that assessment is not just about National Curriculum 'levels' but also about gaining insights into the child's pre-existing model of reality. This raises issues of access, that challenge the assumption that all a learner needs to access the standard curriculum is the right English words. For a young learner from Bangladesh or the Punjab, those lands of great rivers, a study of the water cycle based upon Cumbrian streams may not be hugely meaningful. Young bilingual learners need rich experience, through visits and television and the internet, of the realities upon which our national curriculum is grounded. They also need the opportunity to reflect on experiences gained overseas, and on those of their family and community. A 'multicultural curriculum' used to mean a sprinkling of the cultural icons from various traditions. Once seen as a great step forward from the previous monoculturalism, it was later criticised as 'tokenistic' and caricatured as 'steel drums, saris and samosas'. In various ways, the schools featured in this book are rethinking multiculturalism by developing a curriculum which provides genuine access to learners from different backgrounds, and which enables them to reflect upon and theorise their multiple experiences.

The third source is derived from Derek Edwards and Neil Mercer of the Open University (1987), who have highlighted the clash of cultural perspectives at a different level: the learner's model might differ fundamentally from the teacher's not just for particular experiences and ideas but for entire processes and school subjects.

They distinguish between Common Knowledge and Academic Knowledge, which can operate according to different *ground rules*. This is an important concept to apply to the school learning of children from different cultures. An Urdu poetry recital or a Qawali concert is a warm and interactive event – messier than an orchestral concert. The audience applaud and respond whenever there is a slight pause. Fundamentally different ground rules are in play. The confusion many children in secondary school experience in English lessons over the relative importance of creativity and accuracy is well researched, but it could be that the confusion increases when cultural distances are greater. How does a child deal with the different notions of 'reading' acquired at primary school and in the mosque, when s/he is researching for a school project?

If deep learning is to occur rather than just going through the motions, teachers need to be quite explicit about the purpose of activities and processes. There are numerous examples in this book of teachers making the purpose explicit. Theoretical models need to be established clearly and with multiple references to reality. Self-evaluation and target setting and redrafting must be carefully explained, or they will be shallow exercises concerned more with neat handwriting and handing in work on time than with the quality of thought.

English as an Additional Language: a focus on achievement

Most of the schools featured in this book have a long-established tradition of EAL specialists working in partnership with mainstream teachers to develop strategies for language development. A clear rationale has been established, normally based on Cummins' (1996) progression between BICS (basic interpersonal communication skills) and CALP (cognitive and linguistic academic processing). The former tends to be context embedded and cognitively undemanding, whereas the latter is cognitively demanding and at the same time context reduced. For emergent bilingual pupils to succeed at school, a major leap is needed from everyday communication skills in English to the standard discourses of school learning. Some of the most interesting practices I discovered linked linguistic with cognitive development through various forms of collaborative learning. Activities were designed so that more complex cognitive learning could take place with the help of rich contextual support.

In less developed schools, the two most frequent differentiation strategies for bilingual children are based on a more artificial view of language. Both recognise the importance of language, but misunderstand its processes. They are highly visible but scarcely interactive.

The first strategy attempts to make texts more accessible by means of cloze or comprehension, often forgetting that it is possible for pupils to give the answer without understanding – as I saw when the following extracts were used:

Text: Most volcanoes are near the edge of the world's plates.

Cloze: Most volcanoes are near the edge of the world's p...
(or, in the version intended for more advanced pupils)

Question: Where are most volcanoes found?

17

In the second approach, technical vocabulary is taught by giving verbal definitions, but frequently the experiences which the learner needs, or the more everyday usages which serve as a foundation for the technical vocabulary, are ignored. So, in the study of volcanoes, teachers have to ensure that clear connections are drawn between the everyday and the scientific, between crockery and tectonics, so that the pupils' understanding can be secured. Very often, an academic usage is a metaphorical adaptation of the everyday. Later in this same lesson, I came across two 11-year-old boys struggling with the phrase 'liquid rock'. Besides the conceptual difficulty of rock existing in liquid state (difficult enough for any 11-year-old), these two boys lacked the concept or maybe just the word *liquid*. Eventually, one of the boys suggested it was a sweet, liquorice (which he pronounced *liqis*). A different teacher, who had a more sensitive understanding of linguistic and cognitive development, helpfully built towards the concept by discussing pan handles melting on the stove and microwavable containers melting in the oven.

Simplification and careful structuring are valuable when based upon careful analysis, but there is also a need for more open use of language for learning: for exploring ideas in small groups where bilingual pupils can take risks, moving back and forth between English and the mother tongue if they wish. This facilitates connections between Edwards and Mercer's *common knowledge* and *academic knowledge*. Small group talk provides a situation where pupils can articulate their existing concepts, upon which the teacher can base questioning and intervention, which will then lead towards a more scientific outlook.

Vygotsky (1962, 1978) argues that, with the teacher's help, learners can do today what they will be able to do independently tomorrow. (Bruner's word for the process is 'scaffolding'.) Perhaps the same applies to language and experience. Bilingual learners can understand academic language today if it is accompanied by experience, and will later be able to use the language more abstractly without that support. It is easy to underestimate how much experience is needed. The annual geography field-trip is simply not enough. In National Curriculum history, for example, learning at Key Stage 2 or 3 is built upon the more everyday topics of Key Stage 1. For pupils whose English was very insecure in the infant years, and for recent arrivals, those links and experiences need to be provided again and again. This was a process I was pleased to find in many of the case study schools.

Of course, none of this is the exclusive responsibility of the language support staff, but such specialists are invaluable as a second pair of eyes and ears, analysing texts, constantly monitoring pupils' understanding, alert to alternative strategies. Printed texts in school are distinct on several levels from everyday spoken English, and intervention is needed on all these levels – even for pupils who are no longer part of a regular target or focus group. Firstly the semantic level: bilingual learners may find difficulty not only with the technical vocabulary of school subjects but also with apparently straightforward fictional texts. The ten-year-old fluent reader who has clear literal understanding may have problems at the level of connotations, not really grasping the point of the story because *steed* and *challenge*, or *cauldron* and *black cat*, don't ring the right bells.

Frequently, the syntax of printed texts is different from everyday spoken English. Bilingual learners (and indeed many monolingual ones) find difficulties with the passive voice; with anaphora (pronouns, and also words such as 'thus' and 'therefore', referring back to other words or whole concepts); negative conjunctions (unless, although); or the use of phrases in apposition to explain or qualify. Explicit and timely tuition is needed even with pupils who appear to be coping if bilingual pupils are to reach their potential as independent learners.

Finally, even pre-university students sometimes have difficulty appreciating structures and registers, and so present themselves poorly in essays and exams. Their writing may be unnecessarily abstract, barren, lacking illustration, or alternatively so packed with personal anecdote and response that it appears formless and subjective. These students have a right to learn the hidden *ground-rules* – how, for example, they can frame personal experience as exemplification or proof within more objectively stated assertions.

Classroom pressures often lead to the neglect of such 'lesser priorities'. Yet occasional intervention can substantially raise the achievement of learners who are no longer in regular 'focus groups'. A unified assessment system which extends into these issues, and can be used by language development specialists and mainstream teachers across the curriculum, can help identify these needs.

It is a worrying feature of much Literacy Hour teaching that an explanation of language structures diverts from a search for the meaning of texts, but I also found good examples of metalanguage assisting understanding, particularly for emergent bilingual pupils. However, one area which the Literacy Strategy appears not to have considered very seriously is the nature of reading for information. This skill will assume particular importance if greater reliance is going to be placed on ICT. What are the *ground-rules* of different types of reading?

Many children, having learnt to move fluently in linear fashion through a text, have difficulty adjusting to other reading practices. When she was eleven, my daughter was asked to do a project on some aspect of the Tudors, and chose to study Children in Tudor Times. There was, needless to say, no book with that title in the library or bookshop, but we were able to buy three less specific books about Tudor England, each well presented and illustrated and published for her age group. Neither the contents nor the index listed 'children' as a category, so she had to think through alternatives: school, work, even farming. She then found a good deal of information about Henry VIII's children but, being a good socialist, she chose to reject their lifestyle as untypical. One book made bold statements about the four-poster-beds Tudor children slept in. (On another page, it told us that Tudors ate very well, lots of meat and fish, with huge banquets.) She was shrewd enough to realise that many more probably slept on straw on the floor. With home support, she learnt skills (taken for granted by her teacher) of selection, rejection, collation, critical reading. The advice which teachers sometimes give to 'put it into your own words' is simplistic and misleading; children frequently respond by slavishly working through the text and replicating it into their folder, with some slight paraphrasing.

We saw earlier how the arts can be a negotiation of identities and cultures. The same is true of mature reading, and particularly so for

Asian and other bilingual readers. This is intimately connected with critical reading. With such time in the curriculum now devoted to *literacy*, it is vital that we fight against the simplistic and conformist official model of *functional literacy*, and for a broader and more pluralistic *critical literacy.*

The paradigm shift in the reading process to a more selective and reflective mode is difficult enough for any child, since the ground rules of the process are quite different from those previously acquired, namely the careful progression along the line of print to decode and understand. Making this switch might possibly be harder for children attending a mosque school, for example, where the book is sacred revelation and reading can sometimes mean saying words aloud. On the other hand, in our secular media-loaded world, challenging the authority of the text may be crucial for our personal or collective survival. Being textually critical is a route to being socially critical. In my research, I was able to see some interesting practices in developing the critical literacy of bilingual pupils (see Part B).

Community and culture:
an antiracist perspective

It is widely accepted that a good relationship between school and community is a key feature in school effectiveness. Much of the time, however, this is reduced to a one-way process in which the school expects loyalty and support but pays little more than lip-service to understanding community aspirations. If parents make sure pupils attend school and do their homework, that is enough. Such one-sidedness, in the case of ethnic minority communities, is ungenerous and narrow-minded – in effect, if not intentionally.

A common characteristic of the schools featured in this book is the two-way nature of the relationship and the responsiveness of the school to its constituency. This embraces many different initiatives and practices. Although too slow by far, the increasing number of bilingual teachers and (more frequent) classroom assistants is of inestimable benefit. So too is the appointment of home-school liaison officers, who demonstrate a refined sensitivity and sense of initiative and are constantly redefining their own job.

In many English and Scottish schools, the 'community' is valued in theory but is something 'out there'. The knowledge and skills it holds are not used in the curriculum. Parents and other community representatives are rarely invited into schools to convey their special experiences. This is beginning to change, but slowly, and several of the case study schools provide valuable models.

There has been intense concern in recent years about time lost due to extended visits to relatives in Pakistan or Bangladesh. Unfortunately, travel in high summer is uncomfortable, and brief visits are uneconomical. The schools' concern is justified, particularly when language and literacy are weak or tests loom. But there are few examples of successful practice in turning extended visits into educationally valuable experiences. Pupils are rarely asked to write back, take photographs, draw, record the sounds, contribute resources to school. Such individual work might require more time than teachers can spare, but an experiment could usefully be the subject of an externally funded initiative. One of the EAL services has produced guidance on extended visits. (Vernon 1999 for Leicester LEA)

A strength of many of the schools featured in this book is their role as community schools – learning centres for the whole community. Many more undertake this role than are officially funded for it or are designated 'community schools'. The term embraces a wide variety of practices, from the provision of adult education and space for community events, to pre-school playgroups and toy libraries. The knowledge that their mothers are also taking courses is a powerful influence on young children. In the best cases, the provision is underwritten by a clear philosophy of empowerment.

'Community' is a nice-sounding word. Yet reaching out to the community can also involve a shock, as teachers realise the harsh realities of unemployment, poor housing and racism. The quality of understanding in these case-study schools is definitely not cosy or romantic. Schools are beginning to explore initiatives which will empower young people of school age and beyond to tackle injustice and racism. These schools are, in effect, establishing a model for 'Citizenship Education' which is active and relevant.

Nor do young Asians inhabit a 'community' that is something fixed or singular. They live in a world divided by gender and class as well as race. These divisions intersect with each other and with education in complex and sometimes unpredictable ways. The high levels of unemployment in Lancashire and West Yorkshire, for example, have reinforced the isolation of their Asian communities, although long settled; young men turn to fundamentalist forms of their faiths, and patriarchal traditions are reinforced; the disappointments of older brothers in seeking work influences the educational motivation of siblings; the girls seize upon education with collective determination and their own sub-culture of mutual support, drawing selectively and critically upon modern feminism and with varying attitudes towards traditional culture... and so on.

Unfortunately in most discussions about equal opportunities, *class* slides off the agenda. This distorts our understanding. We should take seriously Gus John's criticism that the equal opportunities movement has left white working-class boys out in the cold, to the advantage of the racists (Macdonald, 1989, p306). When we look again at identities, we need to explore also some positive white working-class models, individual and collective. White pupils also have a responsibility in fighting racism, and working-class solidarity can only be strong when combined with antiracism. At the same time, identity is as much to do with the future as with the past. Could it be that, for the young Bangladeshi boy or girl growing up in Birmingham, finding a place in a multiracial working-class is as important as retaining roots through cultural heritage? We need to work on both at once.

Issues of community and culture are intimately connected with a view of the curriculum. The National Curriculum in England was the result of overt political manipulation and censorship. (In Scotland, there is a greater emphasis on social responsibility, for instance in science and technology, though race aspects are less clearly defined, and there is a gap between rhetoric and reality.) Media studies, recent history, the environment and modern society are marginalised. Despite this, the OFSTED Handbook (1995, p82) argued that 'The curriculum should respond to the cultural heritage of pupils and promote equality of opportunity'. The large print (p88) spoke simply of moral development in terms of 'distinguishing right from wrong' (no vandalism, rudeness or theft, maybe) yet the smaller type (p90) asked inspectors to look out for how schools teach wider moral and social issues, for example, 'the study of warfare; the interaction of people, resources and the environment; and the ways in which science and technology can affect our lives'*. It is difficult to see how this can be achieved by a slavish obedience to the National Curriculum.

There is a need for closer monitoring of the achievement of Asian and other bilingual pupils, but we must not allow what is readily measurable to distract us from what is not. Achievement doesn't just mean examination results – though I would argue that examination

* Regrettably this advice has disappeared from the latest version.

results are boosted in schools where achievement is seen also in social and political terms! We need young people who can lead our society forward 'through change and storm and a calm sea, who are socially aware and morally committed and no one's fool' (Wrigley, 1997 p25). At the time of writing I can only fear that these latter qualities will be much needed in the time ahead, as the hostility shamelessly drummed up by Conservative and New Labour politicians towards asylum seekers could increase racist attacks on old and new settlers alike.

Finally, the commitment to community is linked to the struggle for education. Many school buildings in the inner city areas inhabited by ethnic minority communities are seriously inadequate. The teachers who work in them go to enormous trouble to decorate them and disguise the poor fabric of the building, and vital resources are used up in this effort. The teachers work phenomenally long hours, for which there's been no recognition in the form of higher pay. Indeed, in its place a form of merit payment is planned which will benefit more teachers in affluent all-white schools with higher examination results, and undermine the team-work which is so vital to success. For all the differences which good schools make, there remains an undeniable link between poverty and underachievement, which only a drive for better funding, lifelong community education and the abolition of child poverty will break. A commitment to education and to ensuring equal educational opportunities for Asian and other bilingual pupils is inseparable from the wider political struggles.

Misunderstanding school improvement

Research into school improvement is virtually an industry. Millions of pages have been written in different countries. Yet there are some fundamental questions still to be asked. My own concern, reinforced by the contrasting practice I saw in the ten schools, is that the dominant paradigm in school improvement studies is based on 'control and organisation'. The accepted model, in Britain at least, tends to predetermine the nature of investigations and exclude other ideas. This is reinforced by the political culture in which headteachers, advisers, policy makers, education authorities and consultants are forced to operate.

I first thought of the title for this book when talking to Jenny Dunn, at Seymour Park. We were talking about computers and Norweb's sponsorship of a new type of internet connection – or at least I thought we were – when she suddenly told me about pupils running in-service sessions for teachers and parents. This is a wonderful story of empowerment and is fundamentally at odds with a 'control' paradigm of school improvement.

Now, reflecting upon other interviews and case studies, it seems that this is a recurrent but hidden theme showing through between the lines, rarely articulated. The notion that school development gives pupils the *power to learn* and the beginnings of some power over their own lives; of schools which create *a counter-culture* to the surrounding despair in the communities they serve; of *curricula* which, despite statutory constraints, seek to *connect* with the real lives of the learners; of relationships which enable the learners to *find a voice*; of teachers who gain the *courage and confidence* to explore new ways of managing learning.

The dominant paradigm for school improvement in Britain and particularly in England seldom speaks about these issues. It is based upon *control and organisation*, and its discourse and methodology effectively suppress the other story so that the cultures and actions which truly support achievement are marginalised.

In the reductionist versions of leadership, relationships and partnership with parents already discussed, certain areas are almost completely sidelined. Curriculum is normally regarded as something dictated from outside, which teachers simply 'deliver'. This partly results from the National Curriculum in England and its assessment procedures which seriously distort what is taught. However, even the degree of control which teachers still retain is ignored as of no consequence. A similar silence exists around teaching and learning.

Lists of 'key characteristics' of effective schools are disseminated, which are then read as strings which headteachers must pull in order to transform their schools. Because of the reductionism and marginalisation of what really matters, as often as not these tactical moves just do not work, leaving headteachers disappointed and schools demoralised.

OFSTED's efficiency model of school improvement provides a particularly sharp example. LEAs and governing bodies which have succeeded in bringing schools out of 'special measures' have supposedly done the following:

- ensured *strong* leadership is provided. Many schools ...have appointed a new headteacher just before or soon after the inspection of the school

- taken *vigorous* action to improve the quality of teaching, pupils' progress and levels of attainment *quickly*

- produced and implemented school policy documents and schemes of work

- taken steps *quickly and effectively* to improve pupils' behaviour where this was a problem

...and so on. (OFSTED, 1997)

The emphasis on strength and speed and efficiency suggests a process driven from the top, and has nothing to say about the motivation of the staff to work together in the interests of pupils, to reflect together upon teaching methods. It says nothing about the need to transform the culture of pupil attitudes, nor about the quality or direction of the policies being pursued. The 'Key points' are written in a similar style: tell the staff how bad it is, write action plans, monitor, train.

What follows is all top-down: prepare new job descriptions, monitor progress, write out detailed lesson plans, communicate effectively with parents, and so on. There is no serious thought about the nature of teaching and learning; detail and the vigorous pursuit of objectives is all that counts – which details or which objectives is seemingly not at issue! The communication with parents is implicitly one-way.

We can contrast with this the position of one of the world's leading experts on school development, Michael Fullan (1993):

A sense of *moral purpose* is central to leadership.

You can't mandate what matters. The more complex the change, the less you can force it.

Shared vision, which is essential for success, must evolve through the dynamic interaction of organizational members and leaders.

Change comes not only from realising that something is going wrong but also from a moral and social commitment to pupils, a desire to improve their learning and lives and widen their opportunities for a better future. Action plans and monitoring are only meaningful within a re-moralising and re-culturing process.

OFSTED is right that the headteacher must have 'drive and enthusiasm', but s/he must also personify hope, be willing to take risks, develop social commitment, and help teachers to reflect on internal change in relationship to a changing world outside (Blasé 1994).

* * *

The improvement processes of learning communities are not susceptible to mechanistic analysis of simple cause and effect in one-to-one correspondence. Perhaps we can draw some useful parallels with other disciplines. For example, linguists now understand that utterances cannot be understood simply by looking at the words themselves: their significance can be seriously altered by the linguistic, social and cultural context in which they are uttered – the speaker, the addressee, even the precise time at which they were spoken. Similarly, biologists are coming to realise that there is no simple one-to-one correspondence between a 'gene' and its outcome:

> The ultra-Darwinists' metaphysical concept of genes as hard, impenetrable and isolated units cannot be correct. Any individual gene can be expressed only against the background of the whole of the rest of the genome. Genes produce gene products which in turn influence other genes, switching them on and off, modulating their activity and function. If selection ultimately determines whether a particular gene survives or not, it can do so only in context. (Rose 1998, p215)

The situation is no less complicated for schools, yet there is a constant pressure to simplify in the present climate of 'zero tolerance' of failure (Gray, 1999, p137). The politicians want quick results; they like to believe they can tell headteachers which strings to pull in order to notch up GCSE success rapidly; inspectors revisiting struggling schools must know what these strings are; headteachers must show the inspectors that they have taken certain actions which it is believed will soon bring results... even though it's not quite working yet!

In short, the 'control and organisation' inputs only really work within a school community which *empowers pupils to learn*. We need an empowerment model of school improvement, not a control model.

The power to learn

There are fortunately signs of a paradigm shift, and notably so in studies of schools which are particularly successful in educating ethnic minority pupils, where issues of language, inner-city conditions and underachievement have to be considered together.

The agenda must deal with the quality of leadership and the nature of school development but also crucially with relationships and school culture, with teaching and learning, with the curriculum, and with the community. These are central issues for Maud Blair (1998) and her colleagues in *Making the Difference*, although the team does not in the end develop a pedagogical model. They argue as follows:

Leadership and ethos
A strong and determined lead on *equal opportunities*... The head-teachers had an understanding of, and *empathised* with, the *political and social factors* which affected the *lives of their students*...They *listened* to their staff and to parents.

Relationships in schools
Effective schools listened to and *learnt from students and their parents*, and tried to see things from the students' point of view...They created *careful links with local communities*...

Curriculum entitlement
Effective schools were *sensitive to the identities* of students and made efforts to *include in the curriculum their histories, languages, religions and cultures*...Teachers in these schools drew on student identities to illustrate texts and/or complex concepts... One school encouraged *positive inquiry*...The use of the first language was encouraged for settling in as well as for longer term learning. (Blair, 1998 pp6-9, emphasis added)

Raise the Standard (Green, 1999), a report on schools in a consortium of European cities seeking to raise ethnic minority and bilingual pupils' achievement, shows the importance of a *multi-level* approach involving teachers, parents and the local community. It provides international evidence in favour of an empowerment model. Teachers need to be *interculturally skilled* and to demonstrate to children that they *recognise and value their cultural, faith and linguistic heritage.* Schools need to *engage parents as prime educators,* helping them to improve their own educational level and their ability to support their children's education. The model of language development used emphasises *realism of context* and *well-supported practice in small groups*. There are lessons here for other kinds of school, in different contexts.

There have also been some significant constructive shifts within the mainstream literature on school effectiveness and improvement, involving some key writers in the field.

- More creative and open images of leadership are being presented: for example, Christopher Bowring-Carr and John West-Burnham (1997) write of 'artistry, moral confidence and emotional intelligence'; Louise Stoll and Dean Fink (1995) of 'invitational leadership'; John MacBeath (1998) describes 'seven heresies of headship'; and Jean Rudduck (1991) says we should talk less about the *management* of change and more about the *meaning* of change.

- The importance of pedagogy in school improvement is being taken more seriously. Michael Huberman advises Michael Fullan (1992) to concentrate less on the principal and more on the classroom. In transatlantic co-operation, the team of Bruce Joyce, Emily Calhoun and David Hopkins has just produced one book on school improvement (1999) and one on pedagogy (1997). Bowring-Carr and West-Burnham's book (1997) is subtitled *How to integrate learning and leadership for a successful school,* and they particularly criticise the 'replication' pedagogy as a deep-rooted obstacle to raising achievement.

- The importance of changing the pupil culture is recognised as more complex than simply improving behaviour. Stoll and Fink

(1995) emphasise pupil engagement; Stoll and Myers (1998) speak of 'behaviour management' in terms of 'conflict resolution' and discussions. Jean Rudduck (1991), with her deep understanding that pupils are a key to educational development, quotes Hargreaves:

> Our present secondary school system exerts on many pupils a destruction of their dignity, particularly but by no means exclusively [pupils] from the working class...When dignity is damaged, one's deepest experience is of being inferior, unable and powerless.

- Above all, some serious doubts are being raised about the sense of simply making the present system more efficient without looking seriously at the way society is changing and the futures we wish to create. This debate has been entered by such diverse writers as Fullan, MacBeath, Rudduck, Stoll and others. MacBeath (1998) (quoting Silver) reminds us that:

> Good schools have...trained girls to be good wives and mothers, or ...boys to serve the commercial ethic or the Empire. Good has been an infinitely adaptable epithet, used of schools of many kinds by interested parties of many kinds.

In his fictional picture of a school of the future, Bowring-Carr (1997) points out graphically just how outdated our present institutions are. Fullan (1993) argues for 'moral imperatives' such as freedom, well-being and social justice, and believes that teachers of the future will make their commitment to moral purpose more prominent, active and visible. Rudduck (1991) speaks of school as an institution 'frozen' in time, and that 'thawing' is a necessary precondition of school improvement. Further, quoting Connell:

> In a society disfigured by class exploitation, sexual and racial oppression... the only education worth the name is one that forms young people capable of taking part in their own liberation.

I am not suggesting that these various writers on school improvement share a political perspective, or even that they are internally coherent. Simply that the intellectual tools are around and are available to help us achieve a paradigm shift, so as to develop a more radical and more effective *empowerment* model of school improvement.

PART B – THE CASE STUDIES

Seymour Park School, Trafford, Manchester

Seymour Park is a large primary school close to the centre of Manchester. It serves a mixed population: currently, around 70 per cent of pupils are of Asian origin (mainly Pakistani), around 20 per cent African-Caribbean, and ten per cent white. There are high levels of poverty in the area, and 60 per cent of pupils are entitled to free school meals. It is often hard for families to pursue their daily business in this neighbourhood, where inner-city troubles can erupt into acts of violence that hit the headlines.

Against this backdrop, the achievements of the school are truly remarkable. The school is like an oasis in the city. The atmosphere is co-operative and purposeful, the pupils confident and keen to do well. Even in the limited terms of National Curriculum testing, there is remarkable achievement – Seymour Park's test results in English last year were above the LEA average, and well above the national average. In English, 78 per cent of pupils attained Level 4 or above (only two per cent below the government's national target) and fifteen per cent reached Level 5.

The achievements of the school are naturally wider than this. These pupils develop an attitude to learning that will stand them in good stead throughout life and in a rapidly changing world. They are skilled at using computers and confident in their dealings with adults. This is a school in which eleven-year-olds run IT courses for their parents and their teachers. Maybe the secret to success here is that a culture of learning has been developed; learning now has a very high value and public status among these pupils and their families.

ICT – a technology for social learning

> Some people claim that computers isolate. We use them to bring people together. Here children help others; the older ones tutor the younger; children tutor their peers from visiting schools. As new software is published, it is the pupils who review it. The children are now running training sessions for their teachers and for parents. We help the children to be good teachers, by asking them to plan carefully and consider what the adults will most need to know, and where their difficulties may lie, exactly duplicating the process which an adult teacher might use. There was a wonderful moment last year when a Sikh boy taught his grandfather how to use the internet and access photographs of Indian cities he hadn't visited since he was a child. Word of this spread fast, and we are now seeking funding for a community ICT room, which we hope will evolve into a full-blown community learning centre. (Jenny Dunn, Headteacher)

Developments such as this are so important in helping to relate a diverse community steeped in its various traditions to fast-moving educational technology. A shared intercultural understanding of education is being built on the foundation of a genuine belief in the talents and abilities of both adults and children. In this school community, everyone is both teacher and learner.

The school is rightly proud of its innovative uses of ICT. It has sought out extra funding, taken initiatives and put itself on the map, and this has helped to raise the school's esteem in the eyes of the community. It has welcomed many foreign visitors, to whom pupils demonstrate the equipment, and has been featured in the press and on television. This in its turn has helped to develop pupils' self-confidence. It was actually pupils who first suggested a community ICT facility: 'Mrs Dunn, did you see Gordon Brown's speech about schools having computer centres for the community. We should do that'. The children learn to take initiatives.

Social gains were also made through a video conference link with long-stay patients in the Royal Manchester Children's Hospital. An e-mail link has been established with a school in Sweden.

As a further illustration of the social benefits of ICT, the Head quotes a mother whose son had given her lessons: 'I'd never realised he was such a clear speaker. I've learnt about computers and learnt about my son.'

A learning centre for the community

Parental understanding and involvement has been crucial in the success of Seymour Park. In a recent survey, it was discovered that seventy pupils had been away on extended holidays between December and April. The school recognised the value of extended family links and the benefits of travel but felt that the pupils' progress was undermined when they spoke no English or did no reading or writing for long periods. The Head was taking a tough stand on this, and vigorously persuading parents to accept a four-week limit for such visits, including writing this into a home-school contract.

This was only possible because a shared vision was being built and teachers and parents were working together to raise expectations.

> Parents have greater expectations of their children's success and expect to help in achieving this. We've convinced parents of the need for rigour; we talk to them of targets, and individual target sheets state specifically what we hope parents will do to help. (Headteacher)

This has only been possible because of the strong relationships established by class teachers, who go out into the playground to meet parents at the end of the day. Mothers and fathers come into the nursery to collect children and discuss progress, with the aid of a specially designed Record of Achievement book.

The school is also a centre for adult learning. Local playgroups and teachers have run parenting courses focusing on the role of parents as educators, which over thirty parents attended. This covered first aid and safety in the home and how to deal with difficult children, but also considered such issues as gender and expectations. Parents had certificates presented in assembly, which made an important point about the value of learning. 'We don't just invite mums in to make samosas now – of course we still do that, but a lot more besides.'

Parents and governors are also being involved in writing 'big books' for the Literacy Hour, including books on life in Jamaica and other countries of family origin. Further books are planned in a series 'Our Community at Work'. The school wants to emphasise that every form of work is honourable. The community is increasingly a focus of the curriculum. Books are already in use in the early years based upon neighbourhood visits to the newsagents or police station. A television crew worked with ten-year-olds to produce a video diary of inner-city life, as part of a Health Action project, and pupils were involved in the editing. The structured play in the nursery is based around neighbourhood locations such as shops and phone boxes and police cars. One teacher framed a lesson on distances in Europe with the story of a Romanian refugee he'd met in a prison where he used to teach. The school was responding to its diverse population, including an assembly, during my visit, to celebrate Chinese New Year and an Africa week later in the term. Visits out of school were seen as vitally important in developing pupils' understanding of different environments and cultures, whether the immediate neighbourhood or the seaside or the Derbyshire hills, and a termly fieldwork visit for each class was now the norm.

Teachers are constantly reaching out to the community in order to raise attainment. One eleven-year-old, for instance, was very disaffected, but was clearly a brilliant young footballer, extremely clever on the field, exhibiting great skills and brainpower. His teacher went to watch him play on Saturdays and to talk with his coach. They worked together to motivate him. 'We helped him understand that you've got to have clear goals. There's a lot of glamour in football, but it's also very disciplined. They're fanatical – what you can have for your breakfast, how much sleep, lots of training. It's not like zapping a button to switch the television on.' He ended the year with an above average Level 5 in Maths.

Learning together

When the Head recently asked a government minister whether she was serious about the EAZ (Education Action Zone) affording opportunities for experimentation, she was told, 'You can take risks with anything but the Literacy and Numeracy Hours'. In practice, however, skilled reflective teachers are adapting the national framework to their own school contexts. At Seymour Park, the teachers felt pupils were unsettled by a rapid interchange of activities and have concentrated writing into an extended session each Friday. The daily plenary session has been shortened. Extra staffing is being used to create smaller groups and allow some setting. Teachers are supplementing Literacy Strategy techniques with other more familiar approaches, including listening to some pupils read aloud, and shared reading with older pupils and parents.

Seymour Park teachers had been able to discuss the national projects and focus on their potential for raising achievement. The strongest features I saw which had been drawn from the Literacy Project were the collaborative learning and the more conscious understanding of textual structure.

The Year 1 teachers reported very good progress because of the confidence gained from reading aloud together. This was much more effective for many children than individually struggling to decipher each word; all children now saw themselves as readers. Because six Year 2 pupils were reading the same book, the teacher was able to discuss points with them efficiently, raising their understanding of contexts and more difficult language. (In this book, for example, children going camping get together a 'survival kit'; the teacher was able to explain this concept, and, on another page, ask them to consider why the American settlers travelled in wagons that looked like tents.) When the youngest children in this mixed-age class reported on their work at the end of the session, they were applauded by the others. Big books are now being used for history too; the school is writing its own and texts are being projected from a computer onto the wall.

Even very young children are gaining conscious control of textual conventions. There is clearly a danger in the Government's new emphasis on linguistic knowledge that too much talk about vowels and adjectives can distract from appreciating the story; that did sometimes happen here. On the whole, though, the teachers I saw were beginning to use metalanguage to increase pupils' control of literacy and give them power over texts. For example, a Year 2 class was reading a big book about young explorers going over a rope bridge and crossing a jungle. They were improving the text by supplying adjectives for the forest and, quite explicitly, were understanding how choice of setting can influence future narrative decisions. 'You see, immediately you said snowy, it's changed the adventure.' This would pay off on the following Friday, when children wrote their stories about being lost... the children suggested in a rain forest, in America, in an airport.

They were also discussing their inferences and predictions as readers, which enhanced their cognitive development as well as their literacy:

> Teacher: There's something I really want to know. I want to know how the rope bridge got over this river.
>
> The pupils speculated: People took it across in boats... They could have thrown it... pinged it... shot it with a bow and arrow... They had to climb up the rocks on each side... No, the river used to be as high as the bridge, but it's worn away.

Some of the focus on punctuation and sentence structure was clearly valuable, and very young children responded enthusiastically, saying that ! meant you 'say it with expression', and then reading the sentence aloud with great gusto. It was impressive to see six-year-old beginner readers filling in words which developed and showed their understanding of a structure seen in books but not used in ordinary speech:

> 'I want an ice-cream, please,' said X.

The teachers were very clear about the benefits of a more explicit understanding of syntax and textual structures from an early stage, particularly for bilingual pupils. However, there had not been the time to evaluate everything, and some decontextualised exercises were being set whose purpose was less apparent. A seven-year-old girl struggled to put sentences into the past tense, until I suggested she start with the word 'Yesterday'. She immediately succeeded, proving that she had the linguistic knowledge she needed but that a decontextualised exercise was not the best channel for her to use it.

The empowerment from gaining explicit control over processes was also apparent in Mathematics. A class of older pupils were talking about the solution to a problem of how much change you'd have from £10 if you bought a spade and three plant-pots. The teacher encouraged their alternative strategies (repeated addition; multiplication then addition; rounding up) and discussed circumstances in which a particular method might be advantageous. No blame was placed for getting the wrong answer, but pupils were asked to consider why for themselves: 'Did anyone get a different answer. Let's have a look at that... So you understand why? Has anybody got any questions?' The pupils were confident learners, able to articulate the process. They were also setting greater challenges for themselves and each other; from calculating 3/4 of 64, and 4/9 of 27, they were writing their own questions: 9/8 of 72, 7/2 of 18. They were becoming active learners, not dependent ones.

> Pupil: Miss, can I come up and show you?
> Teacher: Yes...Oh thank you, you are a good teacher.

A school for growing in

The teachers at Seymour Park have worked quite deliberately to develop the school environment. Physically much has changed, due to a thorough remodelling of the building five years ago. The playground provides quiet seating among plants and shrubs, as well as a place to play. The school cat Lady Jane is a familiar figure as she wanders her territory. In the corridors there are photographs of children as active learners, as maturing young people, displayed amongst the tokens of achievement – certificates to show who met the MP, or the curriculum awards won by the school. Alongside beautiful paintings of flowering plants, there are life-sized figures of great achievers and achievements of the past: Mary Seacole and Florence Nightingale, the first man on the moon and the Taj Mahal.

It would be misleading to call the atmosphere 'calm' – that would seem too lacking in activity, in motion. A closer description would be: courteous, purposeful, inquisitive. The Head uses the words 'a tidy workshop, lived in.'

Within lessons, as I hope to have conveyed, and in the life of the whole school, the emphasis is on developing confidence. I had the privilege of seeing the Chinese New Year assembly, performed by the infant classes for themselves and then for the juniors. Unusually, this was not introduced by a teacher but, with remarkable confidence, by a pupil equipped with microphone. No teacher spoke, though one played a recorder to lead her Year 1 class who sang in English and Chinese. Children read poems about social harmony, told stories, portrayed the animals after whom the years are named, and danced in as a dragon. Particular pride was evident among the small number of Chinese pupils and, for the rest, this was a festival in which all could share, where there would be no divisions of religion. Over thirty parents were present, familiar visitors. It was only at the end that a teacher spoke, praising the children and inviting applause for each group in turn. 'Today we were a real team, the Seymour Park team!' She invites children to be dragons when they go out into the yard for break.

The Head and staff understand how hard it is for children from the inner city to succeed in life; they need to develop a sense of purpose early.

> I asked one boy who was always in trouble not why he was in trouble, but 'What do you want to do with your life?' He said he wanted to be a policeman, so I arranged for him to meet the community policeman. I could have talked about my brother, but it was important for him to talk to a Black policeman. I told him he would have to plan ahead, take steps, have a route now.

> 'Eventually, you may decide to do something else, but the steps you've taken will be useful for that too. Do you understand that?'

> 'Well, I've got to start now.'

> 'You need to get fit, to concentrate, to work hard.'

> Sometimes it feels like we're killing childhood, but they do understand.

> I tell teachers that average targets for a class are no use, but it's MY class, they need to know what each child can do, and what they can do better and where they can go. Each individual counts. We're not only opening gates, we're driving them through gates. The struggle is worthwhile but not easy. The children see excitement and glamour through the media, in sport and fashion, but they don't see the long practice, the hard graft. (Headteacher)

Children are encouraged to gain confidence from an early age. An Asian teacher explained how the structured play environment meant children could talk with other children even if too shy to talk with the teacher. The very good pupil-teacher ratio meant that individual needs could be attended to, personalities fostered. The children saw themselves photographed in reading books based on fieldwork visits.

The confidence is combined with thoughtfulness. One five-year-old came to point out to me the huge whale on the wall, as another pointed to Antarctica on a globe. I asked, searching for something to say and feeling rather stupid, 'Is it a kind whale?', not really expecting an answer. A few seconds of silent thought, then, 'I don't think he is. He eats penguins'.

The road to improvement and the headteacher's role

In Seymour Park, there is no contradiction between collegial structures of responsibility and the headteacher's hard determination. The school's mission statement and aims were developed by the whole staff during a residential weekend five years ago, just after the physical remodelling of the school. If this had not been the case, it could degenerate to cliché, empty rhetoric:

> At Seymour Park, we are committed to making the best possible provision for our children, in order that they may achieve their full potential in all activities engaged in by our school community.

The mission statement distils into six major aims, and in each the objectives determine the action plans, ensuring that everything which takes place, whether in the classroom, corridor, office or playground, is directly traceable back to an overall philosophy.

The literacy hour was not simply regarded as new instructions from on high but was actively discussed for its possible benefits, and it is being developed by a staff who share ideas and resources. It is this process which is enabling the staff to take the best from it and alter what does not work: planning a division of activities now across the week, not each separate day; writing their own 'big books'; safeguarding provision for individual reading for pleasure, shared with parents; ensuring time for extended writing, from concern that subskills taught in decontextualised exercises do not transfer; raising concerns about the need of younger children to practice spoken language. Many teachers hold specific responsibilities as team leaders or project managers, leading by example and promoting co-operation. Because the vision is shared, the development processes collegial, the Head can give as the main reason for success: 'staff commitment... determination... teachers focused on each individual child'. Teachers are expected to show progress for each child, through a Record of Achievement shared with parents twice a year.

Headteacher Jenny Dunn is skilled at networking, tapping into funds and initiatives, but clear about educational purposes. She will work with regional television, with the local FE college, providing new learning opportunities for children and parents. She is grateful for the Education Action Zone as a source of additional funding for classroom assistants and mathematics resources but has been concerned that the pressure to show immediate success will undermine it. 'It's supposed to be innovative, but there's so much target-setting that there's no room to take risks. We need teachers to take risks – just instructional methods, transmission teaching, will not work.'

She is keen to see pupils engage in cognitive development, learn to think creatively, to co-operate and show initiative; to participate in group problem-solving and communicate with others, to learn to learn – all the skills necessary to make them employable and successful adults in ten to fifteen years time. Cognitive development has been fostered in some realistic contexts, such as writing and planning the publication of the big books or planning an end-of-term party. In the literacy hour, children are encouraged to see that they can write even better books than the ones they are reading, are asked to speculate on alternative narratives, on what will happen if...?

It is difficult to be a successful school leader in an inner city school in today's Britain. There is a difficult balancing act between protecting children from some of the happenings in the neighbourhood, and welcoming parents to the school; there are dangers – sensitive antennae are needed, an acute awareness of people and situations. 'This was my third headship. It's no job for a rookie.' She has had to stand up to people to protect her children's interests, and is not afraid to create an upset when it's needed. It is difficult to see how Jenny Dunn and the staff find time for philosophical reflection, but somehow they do reflect on a fast-changing world and on how education must change:

> We're doing a lot of thinking about the learning environment, in the widest sense, not just school but in the wider world. We are working on rebuilding communities, but paradoxically also we stress the importance of the individual: both are threatened through some of the cultural and technological changes. The staff understand this, though sometimes at a reactive level. My role is to keep my head above the parapet, above the trees, to drive the vision

With particular thanks to Jenny Dunn (Headteacher), Sue Harrison (Head of Key Stage 2) and Liz Bradley (Head of Key Stage 1).

Rushey Mead School, Leicester

Rushey Mead is a large 11-16 school in the city of Leicester. It takes its students from a mixture of suburban and inner-city terraced houses. Over 90 per cent of the 1200 students have English as an additional language. The majority are Gujerati Hindus (some via East Africa), with a significant number of Punjabi Sikhs and Muslims. About ten languages are spoken by students.

According to the test results for eleven-year-olds, students entering the school are below the national average: the 1999 inspection report states that only 40 per cent had reached level 4 in English, maths or science. Yet the proportion of students achieving 5 A*-C grades at GCSE is above average, at 52 per cent and 53 per cent in the last two years. This is a dramatic improvement from the 35 per cent in 1996. Last year, no student left the school without at least one GCSE pass.

Some schools might be tempted to produce this degree of improvement by means of a hot-house or force-feeding approach. At Rushey Mead, teachers' expectations are certainly very high, but achievement has been raised through generating a high level of student motivation. OFSTED inspectors use the word *excellent* very sparingly, yet this was their headline to describe the students' attitude to learning. The students...

> have a very positive attitude to learning. They are *very interested* in their work, with a high level of commitment and are often *enthusiastic*. They maintain their *concentration* extremely well. They work independently, and *co-operate* very well, and show *lots of respect for one another*. (my emphasis)

Perhaps this last phrase is the key. There is respect for each other as learners and as human beings. This is fostered through the school's pastoral structures, in which teachers develop a respect for students and their achievements, and earn respect for themselves as people.

The respect extends to human beings in the wider community, locally and on a world scale. The school's motto is 'Be Concerned'.

The school's curriculum is rich and empowering. One unusual feature is the *Enrichments* course, lasting two hours each week. In addition, the school has encouraged and enabled students to engage in a wide range of community involvement, including action which directly challenges racism and poverty. This is 'Citizenship Education' in action.

Supporting bilingualism: students and families

Rushey Mead has taken active support for bilingualism very seriously. A growing proportion of the teachers are bilingual, and bilingual assistants support the curriculum in various ways. Gujerati, the main community language, is taught from Year 7 as an optional alternative to French, and the school hosts a supplementary school attended by children as young as seven or eight. Students may sit GCSE in Gujerati at age twelve or thirteen, giving public recognition to their achievement. A part-time teacher provides teaching and comprehensive support for Portuguese speakers from Europe, Africa or India. She supports them directly, helping some to take GCSE in Portuguese, and provides them with advice such as accessing Portuguese television on satellite. Exceptionally high grades are achieved in the community languages.

Across the school, over 100 students are identified who were not born in Britain, and have not had all their education in England. There is a significant number of new arrivals each year from a wide range of backgrounds, including political refugees.

The Language Development Team have recognised, through detailed assessment on entry in English and in the mother tongue, that many students arrive from overseas with limited English but well-established skills and concepts. Against generally accepted practice, students are provided with bilingual glossaries of key words and ideas. For example, a team of subject specialists have worked with the language teachers to produce 80-page illustrated revision booklets for Mathematics and Science, translated into Gujerati and Portuguese. This empowers the students to transfer concepts into English, as well as strengthening first language development.

The local EAL service supports this view in its advice to teachers:

- Encourage students to use and refer to their first language

- Give students literate in their first language the opportunity to make an initial draft of a writing task in their L1 (first language)

- Organise groups so that EAL students who share a common L1 are able to 'think through' a learning task together in their L1

- Provide EAL students with bilingual glossaries and dictionaries if possible.

The school gives much more intensive tuition to newcomers than is the norm elsewhere. The Intensive English Programme provides for this group in a flexible way which is closely targeted to individual need. Initially, the students may spend several days with the team for induction and assessment, after which they are taught in mainstream classes in some subjects, usually Maths, Science, Design and Technology, Physical Education and tutor groups. Since these subjects are strongly supported by language development teachers, new students are able to join these mainstream classes quite early. Humanities and English are usually the last, because of the heavy linguistic and cultural demands for successful learning.

The Intensive English Programme is both a language programme and an accelerated entry route into the National Curriculum. It ensures that students have a grounding in the concepts, terminology and key content of school subjects. Teachers are particularly alert to individual needs: some may lack curricular knowledge, others may have the knowledge but not the English language, and this may vary between subjects.

There is an early emphasis on developing curiosity, in recognition that some students have experienced schooling that uses mainly transmission models, perhaps in extremely large classes.

The team have learnt to be exceptionally adaptable to meet individual needs, and liaise extensively across the curriculum. They are involved in the induction of new teachers, in staff development and in supporting PGCE students. A study club is also provided in lunchtimes for students wishing to consult Language Development teachers; this helps to support homework and independent learning.

The bilingual assistants work for most of their time in subject class-rooms but have a range of other responsibilities. They help the school welcome new parents. They run an interpretation service for parents' meetings, translate and liaise. They explain how the secondary school works, including its structure, curriculum and special activities. The home-school liaison worker for the local schools told me that new students and parents whom she visits before transfer to secondary school always ask, 'Will you be there?' The transition is unusually well supported through the 'Moving On' project; parents are recruited to work with children in the last term of primary and for as long as is needed in the first term of secondary school.

Nationally, there is widespread concern about the educational loss caused by extended overseas visits. The bilingual staff, who are well known in the community, are able to explain that this should particularly be avoided in the later secondary years or if the student's English is not very secure. However, Rushey Mead also recognises the cultural and educational value of these visits and tries to set a work programme, giving students a diary and expecting them to produce photographs. The Leicester EAL service have produced a booklet, 'How to maximise the benefits and minimise the adverse effects of extended visits overseas' (Vernon, 1999), in which suggestions are made about what the students could write about to present on their return. These suggestions are organised in subjects:

- Geography: main towns, rivers, climate, descriptions of the area, transport, major areas of industry, agriculture, fuels used, map-work

- Maths: local currency, comparative costs, salaries, time differences, distances

- RE: major festivals, ceremonies witnessed, special buildings

- Design and Technology: local architecture, famous artists, buildings, handicrafts

- Science: plants, animals, habits, famous scientists.

The bilingual staff emphasise how important it is for the school to recognise and promote the home language. Without this, children and young people are often ashamed to use their L1, and their skills decline rather than progress. The home-school liaison worker told me how, in a previous school, her children had been losing their identity, so much so that they insisted on wearing jeans for a wedding, but that now they took pride in their identity and culture. She had noticed that in schools which didn't support bilingualism, bilingual speakers were so ashamed and embarrassed that they would shun newcomers who shared their home language rather than helping them.

Collaborative learning

There is a culture of innovation and calculated risk-taking across the staff. Language development teachers have particularly supported teaching and learning by developing resources for collaborative learning. This notion involves:

- learning activities which avoid a simple transmission or replication of knowledge

- carefully structured co-operative activities in small groups

- the development of spoken language.

These practices are theoretically underpinned by a booklet *Collaborative Learning Activities in the Classroom*, written by Steve Cooke (1998), who is based at Leicester's Resource Centre for Multicultural Education. Bilingual students need to move from basic communication in familiar contexts (BICS) towards more academic uses of language (CALP) (see Cummins, 1996 and p17 of this book). Thus, challenging ideas should be built on the foundations of a clear context and on the student's existing knowledge and understanding; the process should move from the specific (examples, case studies etc.) to the general (rules, generalisations, concepts, principles). This depends on carefully planned materials and process.

Language development teachers and subject specialists at Rushey Mead have written and developed collaborative activities for a variety of subjects. For example, an extended *Islands* activity developed for English lessons requires students to consider issues such as climate, plant life and wildlife, water supplies and terrain. Students work together to plan the building of a shelter, make a map, decide the characteristics of their companions, work out what they will eat or drink. Not only are specific skills and concepts developed but the students develop a holistic understanding of people's relationships with their habitat and environment.

Part of the skill of planning these activities is the requirement that knowledge be reprocessed through a collaborative thinking process, into a different form or for a different purpose. Thus, for example, the teachers have developed a simulation *Application for the Vacancy of Enzyme*. Job descriptions are drawn up, CVs written, questions for interview planned and undertaken and a successful 'appointment' is made.

Rather than a passive study of evolutionary adaptation, the *Adaptations* activity presents students with environments and with 'starter animals', and requires them to decide how they think the species might adapt to the habitat to ensure its survival. Linguistic support is given for this, focusing on the language relating to reasoning and justification; fantasy animals are displayed in a large chart, highlighting the syntax of causality.

The principle of collaborative work is well embedded in the learning culture of the school. For example, in the French lesson, the speed of reading and degree of concentration are increased by the simple but effective device of posting information around the room, which students hurry to collect and understand in order to solve a problem. This results in collaboration and healthy competition which is more effective than individual reading with 'bottoms on seats'.

Vedic Mathematics activities give opportunities to value Indian culture and discovery, and enable stimulating and open-ended exploration of number patterns and spatial representations in which discussion is promoted through exchange of ideas between groups.

The English lesson I saw was a good example of partnership teaching. The mainstream English teacher and the EAL coordinator share full responsibility for two classes, a partnership which involves planning, teaching together, marking, parental liaison and evaluation. In this lesson for a lower set on the punctuation of speech, the mainstream teacher started with a cartoon with speech bubbles. Firstly, there was a whole-class process in which the students wrote the opening paragraph of the narrative. Then they collectively suggested and explored alternative words and phrases to express how the characters would be speaking: groaned, complained, shouted, said excitedly, and so on. Students were very ready to volunteer alternatives, such as an exclamation, and enjoyed acting out the dialogue with intonation that matched the verb or adjective. This was continued in pairs, using different colours for the two characters and the framing narrative. At this stage, large sheets of sugar paper were used, allowing the results to be displayed, shared and discussed. Thus, a potentially boring practice in punctuation became an active lesson involving issues of narrative and characterisation, in which students were required to discuss their solutions.

There were many unusual features in a Science lesson on bacteria and viruses. A language development teacher supported this in various ways, including ensuring that learners new to English understood the key concept and purpose of each activity, enabling them to contribute their own experiences and observations in whole-class discussion. In line with constructivist principles, the teacher first explored students' prior understanding, the cognitive models they arrived with. He was known for his skill at switching an entire lesson if this initial assessment showed it to be necessary. Students were challenged to explain the differences between bacteria and viruses, their links with disease, the way they spread and multiplied, and so on. There were hardly any closed questions, and many challenges: 'What do you mean by that?... And what will that do?'

When they were told that bacteria divide every twenty minutes, the students were challenged to estimate how many there would be after a day. The teacher clearly enjoyed teasing them: 'Will you need a calculator? Who thinks they might need a calculator?' Students were amazed to see how many there would be by six in the morning or by midday, in an exponential growth resulting in a long line of noughts.

Clear guidance was given for designing an experiment, controlling all other variables while comparing bacteria from two different sources. However, students began thinking creatively, acting as scientists. Individuals came forward to propose alternative experiments, such as testing whether boiling or freezing would kill them off. After appropriate guidance, these variants were encouraged and carried out. This was independent learning but within a collective framework in which theories and processes could be discussed and developed.

Thus, collaborative activities are effective both cognitively and linguistically, and give public status to learning and achievement.

A family atmosphere

Rushey Mead is unusual among state schools in having retained a kind of 'house' system, known as the Divisions. It has been well developed thanks to much reflection and discussion, and it serves the school well.

The structure provides for personal and social education, pastoral and academic guidance, and the need to belong to a visible unit. All students from the same family are placed together in the same division. Teachers also belong to a division and meet with the Division Head at the start of the day. One of these explained that she teaches English to the Year 7 classes in her division, and Enrichments to the rest. She visits each form in turn, gets to know students' achievements in and out of school, tracks progress and liaises with outside agencies to help students with problems.

The division assembly I saw was remarkable. Students of different ages presented their comments on what it is like to be that age, and then a dozen teachers, of various ages, made statements about their own stage in life. Here was a sense of security as students and teachers opened up to each other.

A community curriculum

Great emphasis is placed on spiritual, moral, social and cultural development, to which the PSE programme makes a big contribution. It includes morning sessions with form tutors, an extended two-hour session each week (the Enrichments course), and community activities.

Enrichments is taught by a dedicated and willing team who plan together and are skilled in more interactive and community-based learning. It existed before the national designation of 'cross-curricular themes', and survived their demise. Now the same programme puts Rushey Mead ahead of the field in the new Citizenship Education curriculum.

Enrichments covers the standard areas of PSE such as health education and relationships. It provides practice in study skills, linking this to stress management (dealing with parental pressures, learning to prioritise). It provides courses in parenting. It challenges students to make an active response to environmental problems. Crucially, there is a regular focus on antisexism and antiracism. Students are made aware of their legal rights and encouraged to explore and challenge oppressive structures and behaviour.

Each Year 10 class spends an afternoon a week, for one term, on community service. This provides not only a new social experience and valuable learning of interpersonal skills but also great self-esteem, particularly for students who are not shining academically. Students work with the very old and very young, taking on new roles of trust. Some help at a lunch club for elderly local people; boys work in nurseries, with under-fives who rarely see a male helper; they assist primary school non-swimmers in the water.

Rushey Mead has never had Community College funding but probably exceeds most funded community schools in its range and quality of activities. Disturbing social problems are not hidden from the students. They have helped paint rooms for the new NSPCC building, and designed leaflets for the Leicester Action against Domestic Violence.

The parent governor who leads the Friends of Rushey Mead Association pointed to students' rounded education as a strength of the school. 'They get to think of themselves as people, and their needs as individuals. There are opportunities here to do anything, to get involved politically.'

Youth has a voice

The headteacher and the Enrichments team have given strong support and encouragement to students in articulating and organising around their concerns. This has resulted in unusual skills of leadership and communication, and a number of projects in which students are working for real social transformation.

The school has helped to initiate three national conferences linking students active on school councils in London, Leicester and

Birmingham. These have included workshops on bullying, racism, the school environment, international links, and the need for a more active curriculum.

Rushey Mead students have been actively networking with other schools in Leicester, and have contributed strongly to the development of the Leicester Young People's Council.

A group of Rushey Mead students raised concerns about child labour across the world and the lack of educational opportunities. As well as working with others in school, they have made this a central concern of the Young People's Council, and are actively planning an international conference *Youth Voice* for summer 2001. As a Year 11 student explained, they had begun from the standpoint of the UN Charter for Human Rights but increasingly understood that child labour and lack of education are fundamentally the result of poverty.

Antiracism has been central to students' concerns. They have been able to raise the issue at the Young People's Council. Students at other schools which were about to be merged then felt confident enough to organise a conference to air their own concerns, whether about transport or about the possible problems of a multi-ethnic school merging with one which was seen as monocultural.

The students and staff have been very active in campaigns to stop racism in football. They have promoted the national spectator campaign, particularly at Leicester City, but a group of students also raised the question, 'Why are there no Premier League Asian players?' Football is a central part of British culture, Asian lads are keen players and yet they are denied full participation. This led to the campaign *Eastern Promise*.

In exploring the issues, students began to question their public image and self-image. They designed new kit which reflected Asian culture in its colours and patterns, and had it made by local FE students. As the teacher leading this project explained:

> No one makes it in the game. We had to change from talking-shop to action-shop. Everybody had negative images. Young players had been labelled as 'not up to it'. Looking at images was an important stage in building consciousness. There are no images of Asians in football. We

> are the invisible detail in the 'beautiful game', constructed by those with power and influence. (Tarsem Dhillon, Enrichments Team)

The project was using the arts as a powerful means of ideological challenge. It resulted in a 90-minute show, 'All in the Game', highlighting through drama, comedy, dance and other media the discrimination faced by budding stars, for example during their club trials. The students questioned the stereotypes held of Asians: 'You have the wrong diet', 'You're not aggressive enough', and so on. The video of the show was presented on regional television. Now the participants are wondering whether they should be challenging those who really hold power in the clubs, pointing out that unless they bring the Asian community fully into the game, they are losing major financial opportunities, especially in grounds which are half empty. But what is at stake is clearly more than football:

> Football is central to British culture. The exclusion of Asians from football is a metaphor for all the racism out there. (Tarsem Dhillon)

He also pointed to Rushey Mead students excelling in chess, cricket, basketball. A Year 11 boy was coaching the Year 8 cricket team to a very high standard. The school chess team had beaten England under-18 champions at Oakham, a public school which invests heavily in its coaching. 'Our basketball players beat the team from the local Sports College. But will they make it?'

Making it happen

Steve White has been headteacher of Rushey Mead now for fifteen years. He took over a 'decent school' with some features that were already established, such as the Divisions. He has built on these but been able to innovate and extend. The word 'achievement' is understood to involve a wide spectrum of activities but the exam results provide irrefutable proof that this breadth does not conflict with academic success.

He raised the issue of antiracism right from the start in his first staff meeting, much to the surprise of some staff. This concern was gradually embraced by more and more staff, though some had an entrenched attitude at first that 'teachers are here to teach', and, in his words, there was some 'subtle discrimination' in the school at that time. In fact, discussing racism was crucial to raising achievement. There was racism in the neighbourhood but students had kept their experiences to themselves and had felt unable to discuss them at school. There had been a gulf between school learning and the students' wider experiences.

Since then, they have been involved in many campaigns and the head, a keen Leicester City supporter, has used his many connections and his immense skill at networking to facilitate student initiatives. He is very much a head who 'makes things happen', not as random initiatives but by listening to and supporting the students' own concerns. This is how the *Eastern Promise* campaign about racism in football, and the *Youth Voice* project on children's rights, began.

Steve's metaphor for headship is 'the helicopter mind'. You have to be able to hover above the surface, to see into the distance and get an overview, but then you have to descend and get actively involved in particular projects.

Bilingual teenagers shift fluently between diverse situations and cultures. Steve's spheres of involvement are similarly diverse. He seems equally at home in local corridors of power or on the Leicester City supporters' bus or on a charity bike-ride across India. This breadth is reflected in the eclecticism of objects and displays in his office. His room is a busy meeting point: during my three days at the school, it was used for students to interview Madasan, a pop group visiting to open the new music room; and for a visiting professor of education meeting representatives of Leicester Young People's Council. This connectedness seems unlimited; I walked down the road towards my hotel with the head at the end of the day and we stopped every few yards to talk to people he knew, parents, former students, shopkeepers, members of many organisations.

He emphasised the principle of 'homology': the attitudes among the staff will be matched by relationships between teachers and students; 'it's no use expecting teachers to value and support students unless they feel valued and supported themselves'. The management team know that if you're fostering sustained improvement, you need to empower people to take on new roles and take risks, but you also have to make judgements about their experience, their family and personal circumstances, their health, and know how much they can reasonably take on. As a school community, you develop by learning from best practice, but you mustn't cause resentment by always praising the same people.

Structures have been established at various levels to support improvement. The school has one of the strongest induction programmes for new students that I have seen; the Intensive English Programme for students joining the school from overseas; a well established mentoring programme for older students, and it is now planning to mentor some underachieving Year 8 students. Students are helped to value themselves and seize opportunities – but knowledgeably, so that they don't live in cloud cuckoo land. In a sense, there are parallels at staff level, in development planning: the deputies interview heads of department to explore their concerns and potential areas for improvement and then, rather than leaving the head of department isolated, they will both meet with the rest of the department to continue the discussion and formulate a plan.

The divisions too have their own development plan, based on agreed school priorities. As one deputy head explained, when he first joined the school he had thought the Divisions might be rather old-fashioned, like the 'house' structure of traditional schools, but realised that they were functioning very powerfully 'for the transmission of culture, values and membership. If this is traditionalism, it is a very acceptable tradition, which works to support inclusiveness.' (Adam Newman Turner)

This is a school with a rich culture and spirit. The deputy speculated on whether they had drawn from the exuberant spirituality of Hinduism, with its rich eclecticism. 'The students are always ready to value one another's achievement, and there appears to be no jealousy.' Whether or not this religious hypothesis is the case, the processes at work in the divisional assembly were visibly creating a joyful and buoyant ethos of achievement.

Achievement is a political direction

The staff of Rushey Mead have not had it easy. One of the biggest problems they've had to contend with is the school building: a third of lessons take place in temporary classrooms. This is in itself a form of institutional racism – no school with a mainly white population in the affluent suburbs would have to put up with it. The buildings mean students getting soaked when it rains; they mean no computers in many rooms because they cannot be safely stored; they mean that some of the outstanding foreign language teachers cannot use video or the internet.

The school has had to campaign hard to get the accommodation which should be a basic right. It has taken real determination and corporate spirit not to be overwhelmed by this, but to maintain the focus on raising achievement and creating opportunities for young people. A recent reorganisation of local schools has made things even worse by increasing student numbers, but still the new building is only an architect's plan.

When the linguistic situation and attainment on entry are taken into account, few schools can match Rushey Mead for achievement. Even rarer and equally impressive is the level of community involvement, the culture of thoughtful and forceful campaigning.

This is no distraction from academic attainment – quite the contrary. Firstly, the social involvement gives students the confidence to achieve. Secondly, without this social development, the students would go into the adult world with a clutch of examination certificates but without the skills and ability to overcome the obstacles that society is likely to put in the way of their future success.

With particular thanks to Steve White (Headteacher), Allison Smith, Sarah DuFraisse and Peter Wilson (Language Development), Bhanu Patel (Home-School Liaison), Steve Cooke (LEA Resource Centre for Multicultural Education), Debbie Phipps (English), Chris Mercer (Science), Aruna Kadowala-King and Lucy Gray (Heads of Division), Jean MacDiarmid (Community Activities), Hilary Hay (Friends of Rushey Mead Association), Rahim Sattar (Year 11 Student responsible for many youth initiatives), Lata Samani (Gujerati), Tarsem Dhillon (Science, Enrichments) and Adam Newman Turner (Deputy Head).

Plashet School, East Ham, London

Plashet School is a girls' comprehensive, with over 1300 students. It serves a multiethnic community in East London. Nearly 90 per cent of the girls come from Asian families, and over 90 per cent speak English as an additional language. There is a religious mix, but 65 per cent of families are Muslim. Altogether, 35 different languages are spoken. There are high levels of poverty in the area, and over half the students have a free meals entitlement. However, there are also some better-off families, attracted to the school by its local reputation.

Developing all-round achievement

The school is almost unique and very fortunate in having a Muslim woman as its head. Mrs Bushra Nasir is talented, clear-sighted and ambitious for the girls in her school. After three years as deputy, she took over the headship in 1993. At that time, she felt there was a culture of low expectations and a need to increase the focus on learning, as she was convinced that this could substantially improve the girls' opportunities for a better life. GCSE results were already good by local standards, but since then she has worked closely with her senior management team and the whole teaching and non-teaching staff to develop a school where achievement of all kinds is promoted. Higher level GCSE results have doubled in the past seven years, but achievement is seen in a broader spectrum, including a high profile for the arts. Here, the head has been an influential ambassador, helping to convince parents with more limited cultural perspectives or even religious prejudice against the arts to value this side of their daughters' achievement.

Celebrating achievement of all kinds

Achievement is celebrated in many ways and, very importantly, it is celebrated for its own sake rather than just for extrinsic awards such as merit certificates. There is the annual certificate evening but also much more: the work of the Artist of the Month is displayed directly outside the head's room; there is a Sports Personality of the Term, an annual musical production, recitation competitions, a science quiz. The head leads by example, reading her own work in a poetry event.

The school's work reaches out into the local community: twelve plays, written and performed by Year 10, were taken to local primary schools last year; costumes designed here were used in the Newham carnival. Visiting artists are invited in, and the resulting work appears in the Runga Rung procession, a festival of colour and light, and in venues such as the growing University of East London.

It is interesting to read the notices explaining to students how a commendation can be earned, advice which emphasises crucial learning skills as well as effort and progress. In science, for example, there are commendations for contribution to discussion and initiatives in using the library. Students are commended for uses of ICT that go beyond word processing.

Parental and community links

Links with parents are strong. Last term, over 80 per cent of Year 10 parents attended the parents' evening. Direct parental involvement is normally more difficult in secondary schools but every effort is being made. A small but dedicated parents' group are currently planning an international evening, a summer fayre and a trip to France. (Three coachloads went last time.) Parents helped develop the courtyard, decorated with mosaic, which serves as a seating area for Year 11 students. Successful curriculum evenings have been organised to inform students and parents about curriculum issues and how parents can assist their daughters.

A shared vision and responsibility

School development is shared and purposeful. The senior team is extremely able and many heads of department are very experienced. Early on in each conversation with staff, it became apparent that collegiality and professional reflection are rooted deep in the culture of the school. Seven years ago, the senior team came to certain conclusions: that the school was achieving respectably but could do more – they needed to *promote* achievement; that they could do more to actively *celebrate* the multicultural community within and around the school. They deliberately kept their findings to themselves, so that the whole staff could explore issues and formulate a new mission and aims, as a focus for future development.

On this basis of common ownership, staff are able to accept a monitoring process which places a burden of responsibility on departments to evaluate and report on recent developments, including examination results.

As their side of the bargain, the senior management have been able to secure improvements in working conditions and the appearance of the school, despite a basic fabric which is ageing and, in parts, seriously inadequate. Corridors have been painted in a variety of pastel shades and decorated with stencils. There is a rich display. Teachers receive help from technicians in mounting displays but, for their part, have to change displays regularly, and must reflect the work of the full range of students, not simply a few higher attainers. Improvements were made in classroom accommodation and resources, within the building's limits. Clearly, some areas have been beyond remediation, for example the craft and design rooms, which made me wish the government would put its money where its mouth is.

Many teachers are regularly involved in curriculum planning meetings. These include whole-school working parties with representatives of the different departments, in which good practice is shared; current groups include teaching and learning, special needs, literacy, the healthy schools initiative, and more able students. In the latter, the school is linked to a five-city initiative around *Excellence in Cities*. Another powerful mechanism is the partnership of EAL teacher with mainstream subject teacher; together, over a period of two years, they will plan schemes of work, team teach and evaluate.

The degree of dedication in this school's staff is hard to match, both in terms of the thought put into planning teaching, and staff involvement in special events. When you ask parents or students what makes the school a success, they say the hard work of the staff, but frequently the teachers say it's the students! They appreciate their attitude to work and their receptiveness and attention, but this has not arisen by magic. The extra-curricular events and the residential experience in Year 7 requires much staff dedication but they do cement relationships between teachers and students from an early stage.

It would be wholly mistaken to apply a deficit model to the school; just because this is a predominantly working-class area and because many parents' had limited educational opportunities, that doesn't mean that parents lack ambition for their children. Quite the reverse. They are determined to give them the best possible opportunities. And despite a family culture which is often patriarchal, deep pride is taken in girls' achievements.

Promoting the achievement of girls

Many of the teachers, men and women, like working at Plashet because they are able to give the girls their full attention and develop their confidence and language skills without the boys who so often succeed in grabbing all the attention. Whatever one thinks of single-sex education, this is certainly a feature of the school's culture.

There is considerable emphasis here on building confidence, and in some respects the school's ethos is within a tradition which is common with many independent or selective girls' schools. Prominently displayed outside the deputy head's room is a poster of famous women, great achievers in their different fields, and this theme is often echoed in assemblies and on the daily notice board at the school's entrance. Although I was personally uncomfortable with some of the messages conveyed in it, I was seriously impressed by the confidence and maturity of the young woman, a recent student, who led the Muslim assembly.

The curriculum

The constraints of the National Curriculum are acutely felt in some areas, and a staff such as this deserves greater freedom. Thinking about the students' experience and needs, I wondered why there is little local history, for example, and no study of migration into the East End of London. However, within the official parameters, the school has struggled to relate officially demanded knowledge to students' real lives and to use curricular opportunities to promote their personal, social and cultural development. The creative and performing arts play a prominent role, developing confidence and creativity but also providing a space within which the girls can explore meanings and perspectives and shape their vision of the world.

The school places cross-curricular emphasis on linguistic development in English but also, for many students, develops the other languages of the home and the community. Bengali and Urdu are offered as alternatives to French from Year 7, and other languages are supported for GCSE entry through twilight classes in Panjabi and Gujerati.

The school culture: *a cultural school*

Any visitor who thinks that culture in the East End of London means a sign outside the 'Queen Vic' would have a shock! Cultural values pervade Plashet School. At every entrance, on every stair, there are original stencilled decorations, plants, artistic displays, signs of the school's involvement in community events. The school contributes to the rich local culture and, in turn, draws upon its opportunities.

Art

Art is a particular strength. In the main art rooms, a massive central display, rich in colour and texture, is an inspiration and central focus. The display is changed each term, and during my visit the focus was on decorative arts, from wallpaper and fabrics to carnival costumes. Students concentrate hard on detailed first-hand observations in their sketchbooks, which form a basis for expression in a wide range of media. An artist-in-residence attached to the Docklands Project was working with girls on the built environment, and classes had recently been to the University of East London's exciting new site. Alongside this, students were studying Gaudi and Mackintosh. The talented Head of Department, whose costume designs were shown at the opening of the 'Dome', is constantly aware of community opportunities; the art room is full of signs of this involvement, including glass fibre elephants for the Runga Rung (festival of lights) procession in November.

A central event of the school calendar is the Year 9 Arts Week. Students choose from a range of special projects. They work on it intensively for the whole week, and the work leads to a very real outcome at the finish. These have included:

decorating a central courtyard with mosaic

designing and parading carnival costumes

producing a web magazine

preparing scenery for the school musical.

As in many areas of the curriculum, the art rooms and resources and guidance from teachers are available to students at lunchtimes, after school and on some Saturday mornings. The staff work closely together and the students take an intense pride in their work. Even parents who are initially sceptical about the value of art in either personal or career terms come to share in that pride when they see their daughters' work in the annual exhibition.

Music

Other departments too break the conventional cultural expectations and provide wide opportunities for disciplined creativity and expression. A music teacher told me that when he began at the school, he was led to believe that 'the girls might be too embarrassed to sing in front of a male teacher'. Now there is a thriving musical culture, with regular performances at assemblies and outside events. The annual production is often a musical (last time, Bugsy Malone, with all-girl cast!) and, challenging Indian Sub-continent gender stereotypes, there is also a drumming club.

Drama

Drama lessons are often linked to the plays being studied in English. I was able to see a class of Year 9 girls improvising an extra scene to *Romeo and Juliet*, a scene following the father's angry outburst at his daughter's rejection of a husband. This improvisation consciously gave voice to the three women in the play who are marginalised in the main action: Juliet, her mother and the nurse. This was an important opportunity not only to develop self-confidence and powers of dramatic expression but also to explore situations which are a real concern for some.

English

English and English Literature are central to the girls' cognitive and conceptual development at Plashet. A major strength of the department is to exploit the students' openness to language development and ideas, in order to access a rich and varied range of texts. This is in the best sense a *cultural heritage* model, but with texts chosen for relevance to students' own lives and experiences.

Thus, classic plays like Arthur Miller's *A View from the Bridge*, with its discussion of immigration and the conflicting codes of conduct of cultural groups, make for exciting, accessible and relevant reading. The achievements of the department over the past eight years derive from this extraordinary sense of strength and power the girls feel when studying texts they clearly enjoy. This includes the study of Shakespeare, commended by OFSTED inspectors as 'outstanding'.

Romeo and Juliet, The Merchant of Venice, Othello and *Macbeth* are studied because the plays deal with real conflicts. They are read in an interactive way which encourages students to explore these meanings. Conflicting understandings of family and love are live issues for many of the girls; racism and the limits of justice and revenge are explored through *The Merchant of Venice*.

Because of their openness to and interest in language development, deriving from their multilingual abilities, the students are very willing to engage in the wide range of challenging tasks used by English teachers to develop students' knowledge and understanding of texts. This is a key strength, and allows teachers to value each girl's achievement and contributions so that their confidence is increased across the curriculum. The English department has always worked in close partnership with the EAL department to achieve this confidence-building.

Towards spiritual and moral maturity

The school recognises the mix of faiths by providing separate religious assemblies for Muslims, Hindus, Sikhs and Christians on two days each week, supported by local places of worship, in addition to the multi-faith assembly run by the school staff.

Islam, like many Christian churches, places strong emphasis on scripture as divinely inspired. One major problem, understandably, is that the scriptures were written in a different era and this can create difficulties in finding a straightforward application or meaning for certain passages in the modern world.

In a sense, the central task of religious education in such a school, and of the spiritual and moral development of students, is its response to this disjunction. There is serious danger that unless students are enabled to reflect upon their beliefs, they will grow up living in separate divided worlds, both socially and within their own minds.

During a brief visit, I was able to catch a glimpse of how the school set about providing occasions for personal reflection. In a Religious Education lesson for Year 10, students were asked to research into a present-day environmental problem or issue such as global warming or endangered species or vegetarianism. Each group also had to explore the scriptures and beliefs of two major religions and to come to an understanding of what that religion had to say on this issue. This was by no means straightforward but was a major cognitive and spiritual leap, since students often had to infer or judge the spirit of what had been written centuries ago. I put to the class this problem, that at the time of Jesus or Mohammed, neither global warming nor the extinction of species was an issue. The students readily engaged in a philosophical discussion about how religions based on sacred texts could be related to new problems.

There had been similar work in Year 9 classes, which had been asked to present a personal creed. After reading the Apostles' Creed, extracts from the Q'uran and other creeds, they had to express in words their own beliefs, which they did most thoughtfully, as these three examples illustrate:

I believe in one God because I was brought up that way.

I believe in the holy book and the prophets.

I believe in the day of judgement...

I believe that men and women should be treated equally...

I believe that disabled people should be treated with the same respect as others, they should not feel like an outsider.

I believe in one God,

   Not from any religion, not from any caste,

Just one God, who rules us all.

I believe in the big bang

   And that God created it

So that humans had the chance to live a life.

I believe that nothing is impossible

   And that everything can be done

Maybe not today but definitely one day...

I believe there is a god but he does not control us.

Instead he guides everyone towards the right things.

I believe in Evolution. It does happen

but very slowly so we do not even notice it.

I believe that everyone is equal

No man is higher or lower than anyone else...

These girls are clearly seeking to reconcile different world-views and the knowledge and understanding arising from different sources. Their ideas are marked by reflection, spirituality, moral judgement and a real belief in equality.

Language and thinking: accelerating cognitive development

There has been intensive planning and implementation in many subjects, often achieved through partnership between an EAL and a subject teacher. Such partnerships can last from one term to two years; they are characterised by weekly meetings, team teaching and careful evaluation. Sometimes it is possible to compare results with a 'control group'. The amount of time involved may seem high, but a detailed plan and bank of resources are created for others and the impact on students' learning skills may well be cumulative.

History

In History, a good foundation was laid ten years ago when the National Curriculum was introduced. A network of teachers from five local schools shared in planning and resource development to cover the required units. However, the Head of History and the principal EAL teacher decided to focus strongly on cognitive development and on the interrelationship between language and conceptual development. Each week's work was replanned, by identifying key words and concepts, thinking and learning skills, and a learning activity. Some examples will make it clearer:

Roman Empire

Aim: To find out how Rome was ruled.

Key concepts: government, monarchy, republic, empire, citizen, similarity and difference.

Activities: matching meanings to key words, working out chronology of types of government, writing information on time line, including how change was made, comparing republic and empire, worksheet to support construction of model answer.

Thinking and learning skills: compare and contrast, change over time.

Medieval Realms

Aim: to show the importance of the Roman Catholic religion and the Church in people's lives.

Key concepts: church, Roman Catholic, Pope, bishops, priests, heaven and hell.

Activities: reading textbook account of importance of religion to common people, completing diagram of Church organisation, listening to extract from Dante's Inferno, drawing pictures for display of heaven and hell, writing an advert and job description for a parish priest (two starter sentences in writing frame).

Thinking and learning skills: generalising, rank ordering, interpreting from pictorial, literary and historical sources.

The Making of the United Kingdom

Aim: to begin to understand why people took the side of King or Parliament in the Civil War

Activities: note taking; given family role cards, by which to introduce themselves and debate which side they will support; role-play – a dinner table scene when news of the impending war arrives, plan speeches.

Thinking and learning skills: decision making, inferring, group work, role-play.

Many teachers working with bilingual students will emphasise the definitions of keywords, and display them prominently on the walls. Here the process is much more active. For example, after watching a video, students were given a textual description of a castle and asked to work out on an unlabelled drawing which part was which. Another characteristic is the richness of resources, including many audio-visual representations designed to extend students' knowledge and understanding and often compensate for limited first-hand experience.

The major concepts are ones which are important in understanding the immediate topic but also have strong transfer value into other areas of history and to the students' wider curriculum and cognitive development. Students were learning general skills such as forming and testing hypotheses, evaluating and interpreting evidence, and justifying an opinion. The activities involve active learning, with frequent role-play: they are intellectually challenging and are particularly language-rich. There was also a frequent emphasis on structuring ideas, such as sequencing the sentences in scrambled paragraphs.

Teachers had high expectations of the students' attention and understanding and were not afraid to take risks in presenting texts which would normally be considered to be beyond students' reach. Accordingly they found that extracts from Dante were the best way to convey the medieval image of the afterlife and the strength of religious belief and world-view. Focused listening alternates with reading, in developing understanding.

The head of History informed me that the EAL teacher was not afraid to ask questions and challenge existing practices, and it was clear that a strong partnership had been established, based on trust, self-criticism and high professional standards.

Geography

The planning in Geography has also focused strongly on linguistic and cognitive development. These teachers, like many at Plashet, have made good use of appropriate theory and literature, with the key book being *Thinking skills in geography* by David Leat (1998). Work in pairs and small groups is the norm, and written presentations are frequently displayed. After an exploratory stage working in pairs, students are expected to present and justify their findings to the whole class. Geographical knowledge and information is frequently related to students' lives and experience, leading to a deeper learning and more personal understanding and response.

When considering the effect of global warming, students had to write a 'letter from the future', in which someone living in 2030 describes the climate and their life and indicates how we could have made their future better.

When studying a graph of population change over the last century, students were asked to place biographical and social statements on the graph, such as 'Fewer children share a bedroom', 'Grandparents are very rare' and 'People are encouraged to emigrate to the colonies'. They then had to decide whether each event was a cause or effect of the change in birth or death rates. This work generates a great deal of debate and discussion.

Writing frames were frequently used to support and structure extended writing, but there had been a shift away from starter sentences and large gaps towards starter questions, especially asking about cause and effect and issues to think about. When studying the Kobe earthquake in Japan, students were asked to consider how some of the deaths could have been avoided.

The Geography teacher has worked hard to develop a meaningful curriculum but feels constrained by the compulsion of the National Curriculum. However, the Year 7 classes are able to do a comparative study of Bangladesh, where a significant number of students have relatives and have visited. In a more open curriculum, there would be less worry about 'covering the syllabus' and more opportunity to draw on students' and parents' knowledge.

Science

Although the Science department has, for various reasons, worked less frequently with the EAL specialists, a collaborative and reflective culture within the department and a dedication to learning and achievement has helped the teachers focus on styles of teaching, with a similar emphasis on linguistic and cognitive development.

In the lesson I saw, scientific activities and knowledge were constantly rooted into everyday experience. The teacher demonstrated ways in which kinetic and heat energy accelerates a change in baking a cake, as in chemistry: 'Look. There's almost no difference between chemistry and cooking. Instead of mixing ingredients to make something, we call them reactants.'

The Head of Science was aware of the need to relate technical language to experience and to use all the senses in demonstrating a point. She asked students to break up models of two molecules. 'What did you use? Energy.' To clarify 'exothermic' reactions, she called upon their knowledge of other words with the same prefix. She also showed how some 'activation energy' was used to begin a reaction, such as kinetic energy to start a match burning, pointing out that she was being 'active'. Students were challenged to think through processes, to consider what conditions were necessary conditions for things to happen, and what was happening that we might otherwise discount or overlook: 'We all know that energy is stored in that match. So we just wait for it to come out?'

Another interesting feature of the lesson was the attempt to use absolutely central concepts to structure the learner's cognitive development (a kind of 'advanced organiser', to use David Ausubel's term.) Thus, she compared similar processes in different areas of science so as to strengthen an understanding of energy flow from high to low until equilibrium is reached. She brought together experiences of heat moving from hot metal to cold water, electricity moving to earth, the wind generated by a difference between high and low pressure systems, and so on. In science, as elsewhere, very high expectations of cognitive development were realised through being carefully structured and grounded in everyday reality.

Conclusions

As for all the schools in this book, it would take far more space to tell the whole story. This chapter can only describe and highlight some of the key features of what makes Plashet so effective. An ethos of achievement, in which successful learning is the norm and a source of great personal satisfaction to the girls, has been developed in so many ways:

- learning activities which have a very public and shared outcome, in performance, events or displays

- the concentration and focus of the learners and the quality of purposeful cooperation between them and with their teachers

- the dedication of teachers and other staff, and their satisfaction in promoting high levels of achievement

- the many ways in which success is shared with parents and how well mutual understanding is built up

- the consciousness that education leads to personal satisfaction and development but also to unexpected opportunities for the individual and new possibilities for a disadvantaged local community.

The Head and Senior Management Team make careful use of data in raising awareness of development needs, but not through a culture of fear. The whole-school development has depended upon a shared vision, a collegial responsibility and ownership and dedication. Particular, and intensive, development processes have been adopted which have taken improvement right to the heart of the learning process and which have had a tangible outcome in the classroom.

Though working within a tight national structure, the staff have built up key strengths in the curriculum which related to a vision and set of moral and social values: spiritual, moral, social and cultural development; powerful language development; and intellectual rigour in tackling living issues.

With particular thanks to Bushra Nasir (Headteacher), Ashia Oozeer (Art), David Rollason (Religious Education), Pam Goldup (History), Ranjna Dudhia (EAL), Pauline Gailliard (Geography), Gerry Courtney (Science) and Sally Walker (Deputy Head)

Grove Primary School, Birmingham

Grove Primary School is a large school with a family atmosphere, situated in Handsworth, Birmingham. It has nearly 700 pupils but the size is rarely apparent, as pupils spend most of their time with their own age group in their own part of the building. The older children are based in a new building across the road. The result of amalgamation of an infants and a junior school, numbers are gradually being reduced to three classes per year.

The school is culturally rich and diverse. About two thirds of the children come from non-European backgrounds, including nearly half from families originating in India, Pakistan or Bangladesh. Ten per cent are African-Caribbean and there are some Chinese, Vietnamese and African children.

The school is in many senses inclusive and very much a community school. About half the pupils are known to be eligible for free meals, and many more are believed to be so. Because of its reputation, Grove also attracts some pupils from the more expensive suburb of Handsworth Green. Some pupils from other parts of the city who have had serious difficulties in other schools are placed in the Behaviour Support Unit, and are gradually assimilated into the mainstream classes at Grove. In addition to the nursery, there is a community room, where a playgroup is supported by a pre-school worker jointly funded by the school and local churches: the children attending come to join in school assemblies. There are courses for parents in the school and a hostel for the children out in the countryside. Children take part in short courses at the Children's University, established on the initiative of the former head David Winkley.

A talented staff team

The school management have worked hard over the years to recruit a team of governors and staff who reflect and can respond to the school's diversity. A third of the teachers and over half the teaching assistants are Asian or African-Caribbean, and between them speak and support a range of languages. The head is now keen to find Bengali and Vietnamese speakers. Many of the staff have strong roots in the local area and in Birmingham's diverse community. Students and supply teachers have been well supported in the beginning, and later often invited to submit applications for posts in the school. This is a talented staff. The school has the reputation as a 'training ground' where enthusiastic staff are fostered and develop rapidly to take key positions in the school or elsewhere.

Teamwork is strong. A deliberate effort has been made to recruit teachers who are not only competent in the 'core activities' but can also offer something more. The staff currently includes a former actor, an art graduate, a former scientist. Teachers pass on their special interests and talents to children beyond their own class through team teaching with the class teacher (in the case of younger children) or by exchanging classes (older pupils). Over a two-day visit, I saw:

- the technology co-ordinator team-teaching very young children with their class teacher

- a special needs assistant teaching ICT to several classes

- a teacher giving lessons in jazz dancing to various classes.

Some teachers were looking forward, though not without apprehension, to a dance workshop for teachers at the Royal Ballet – a requirement before the professional dancers will visit a school.

Teams meet for planning and to share ideas at every opportunity. Within twenty-four hours, teachers of Years 5 and 6 had met during assembly time and after school, and found time for a production team meeting to run through ideas for the school musical! On the next day, some staff were managing to fit in a parents' evening, starting at half past four, and then going out to celebrate a teacher's birthday. Not surprisingly, they found the Secretary of State for Education's idea of extending school time to five o'clock somewhat insulting!

The teamwork is upheld by a leadership network spanning the school, including two deputies, phase leaders (each having a curriculum area and a year group) and other year and curriculum leaders.

The head, Pamela Matty, is able to draw on her colleagues' enthusiasm, while realising the need to support and foster them. In her words, 'The school's culture for the children is built on its culture for the staff'. On our tour round the school, she pointed out some team-teaching designed to model a teaching method; this was a frequent practice when someone felt they had a particular difficulty. This is a far cry from the stick-and-carrot politics favoured by some politicians. She and her deputy had recently had occasion to benefit from this culture of team support. During the head's maternity leave, the deputy as acting head was supported part-time by the previous head David Winkley, sometimes on site and sometimes over the phone. (David still teaches at the school one day a week, while devoting most of his time to the National Primary Trust and the Children's University.)

Parents as partners

Parents too are part of the team, as a result of initiatives stretching back over a long time. The school yard is a key meeting point. As a minimum, the year head always goes out into the yard at the end of the day to chat to parents and for informal consultations.

The school seeks to ensure that all parents are involved. Parents' evenings take place three times a year. *Inspire* workshops, at class level, involve mothers and fathers in making educational games to take home. This LEA initiative serves a number of functions, including involvement in the school, quality time with the child, and fostering a greater understanding of the educational value of play. Parents are involved in celebrations, parties and school trips. They are encouraged to attend Friday assemblies, led by a class of pupils. There are also coffee mornings on Fridays.

The Community Room is used for a variety of purposes. It houses the playgroup and the pre-school and after-school clubs. It is a base for training programmes for parents, some of them run in conjunction with the local college. These have included parenting courses, computing and basic maths. Once parents start a programme in their child's school, their confidence increases and they often continue by attending a college-based course. For example, one parent helper became a classroom assistant and is now a trained counsellor. Some are paid a modest wage by the school to help run events or activities: one parent, for example, is now running the *Inspire* programme. Some of the relationships have been long-lasting. The SEN specialist has been involved with the school for twenty years, as a parent, a governor and now a member of staff.

Parents are involved in practices such as shared reading at home. They are encouraged to let the school know about their children's interests and activities. For example, the Helping Hands project encourages children to be more responsible citizens, and any parent can nominate a child for the Helping Hands award.

Respect!

This word, adopted from Black American culture, has taken on a resonance in the school. It is symbolic of the relationships between the adults and children.

The older pupils were in an assembly about the Hindu festival of Holi – a subversive festival in which people can let off steam and be rude to those in authority. There was strong participation. Pupils contributed their understanding of the festival: 'You can talk to your parents!.. It's the harvest...You throw coloured things...You have fireworks'. The teacher reads aloud a text explaining that you can be rude to the people you normally have to show respect to. She asks who are the people you have to respect. The children mention different people – parents, a policeman, your boss at work – and one boy wittily contributes, '*Me!*' 'Yes!', says the teacher, 'we do respect you. We have to respect everybody, and we have to respect ourselves.'

She continues by telling a story of three bears, Tiny Bear, Helpful Bear, and Bully Bear. It turns out that Bully Bear is actually very lonely. Helpful Bear goes after her to ask her if she'll come to play. 'Nobody plays with me, because I'm not very nice. I don't think

Tiny Bear will want to play with me.' Helpful Bear persuades Bully Bear to say sorry and join in the game, and suggests she take a new name. (After this, the teacher lets them know that a child had come to her door feeling very upset...)

This tale of mediation is symbolic of the mature roles some older pupils take on. During the lunch break, a number of children are wearing canary yellow baseball caps. These are the play-leaders and the peer mediators. Both groups receive training, including learning some traditional games of various cultures. Some mothers have helped by teaching the Punjabi games and dances they played as children. The play-leaders and mediators are rewarded by special stays at the school's hostel.

The hostel was the brainwave of the previous head and is now run as a trust serving several inner city schools. It gives children the opportunity of residential experiences to get out into the countryside, to pursue fieldwork for Geography, History and Science. It must play an important part in building relationships in this enthusiastic and harmonious school.

There are bound to be children who behave anti-socially, but an ethos has been created which discourages such behaviour. The school has 'expectations' rather than rules and these have been worked out with the children. In one classroom, the children had drawn posters of their own expectations, again not framed as rules: 'We always look after our classroom. We always work hard...' I also saw a more specific statement of expectations by the teacher of the advanced literacy group and, vice-versa, the pupils' expectations of their teachers!

- to mark our homework

- to always challenge us

- to help us when we need help

- to always be ready to teach us.

When a pupil's behaviour is under close scrutiny, care is taken to set manageable targets and to build their self-esteem. Instead of a report sheet, there is a 'target card'. The target has to be positive, such as 'respect other people', not negative, such as 'don't hit anybody'. The target card is also specific in its focus, and teachers take care not to write about other problems on it. The pupil has to know s/he can achieve improvement on a specific issue.

The respect for children as learners is marked by displaying their work – everywhere: in the classrooms and the hall, on the walls and suspended from the ceiling, on 'washing lines' in the nursery classes. Children's photographs appear frequently, showing the school's esteem for them. Recently, the children were asked to write their thoughts about the school and their hopes for the millennium. These offerings are full of concerns for the future, for the environment, about poverty and war, about local and global problems. These too are displayed everywhere, again showing respect for the feelings and concerns of these young people, citizens in their school and citizens of the world.

'Respect' is also the name of a campaign to raise the aspirations of Black pupils, and overcome racist stereotypes. A poster is displayed of a Black scientist, shaven headed, standing tall and smiling. The caption: 'You don't have to look like a scientist, you just have to think like one!'

The Children's University likewise raises self-esteem as well as raising aspirations and providing additional opportunities for learning, on Saturdays and school holidays. The ethos is of learning, concentration, high expectations and achievement, but not in a hothouse environment. I asked children what was good about the school, and they said 'Friends... Be proud of yourself... Fun'.

The curriculum – a cultural celebration

The creative and performing arts are a major strength of the school, which the teachers are determined to protect despite the drive to concentrate on literacy and numeracy. The rich displays provide reminders of festivals throughout the year.

All the way round each of the three halls are displayed full-size paintings, placed there for the annual art competition. Autumn term ends with a big music festival, for which every class composes and performs a piece of music. The religious festivals of different cultures are celebrated. Pupils enter the city's poetry competition, and a story writing competition is being planned. There is an annual drama production, and a good many sports activities. The competitions are presented as invitation, not duty, but participation is widespread and enthusiastic.

A range of music is enjoyed, taught by experts and enthusiasts on the staff and from outside. A teacher provides jazz dancing lessons to many classes; Asian musicians come in to teach their classical tradition. The Royal Ballet will visit next term. During my visit, a drummer and dancer were teaching West African dancing.

The staff at Grove have not lost the ability – an ability that is fast disappearing elsewhere – to interrelate experiences and learning in different 'subjects'. The dancing is preceded by a reminder of the kinds of things made in West Africa, with a display of woven cloth. African-Caribbean children are reminded of the banny cakes made from cassava – a recipe taken across by the slaves transported from West Africa. It is related to a study of the history of Benin and the geography of the rainforests.

Pupils learn to value cultural and linguistic diversity, and their own bilingualism. They listen to stories in two languages, sing songs in English and Panjabi, come to realise they're lucky to have two languages. They're encouraged to write about their travel experiences. Travel by the staff is also encouraged, and some were recently given leave of absence to visit India.

The learning is frequently characterised by real outcomes. The nursery children had planted daffodils, now displayed, and were making sandwiches with the cress they had grown. Older pupils' articles had been published in *Primary Life* and the *Times Educational Supplement*. Competitions include one for design and technology and one for science, in which pupils, according to their age, pose a number of scientific questions and find the answers to them. In the computing sessions, pupils were developing word processing skills by improving the presentation of their own writing; the next week, they would focus on fonts and colours to design labels for their classrooms.

This is a far cry from the sterile outcomes of our policy makers, for whom nothing appears to matter unless it can be measured. Ironically, this school is doing very well in terms of SATs and has almost doubled its scores over recent years. It would be dishonest, though, not to reflect a tension felt acutely by the Primary 6 teachers, who feel that national policies are driving them towards an imbalanced curriculum.

Achievement for all

In its inspection report, the school was strongly praised for its attention to individual needs. This was evident even during my short visit. I was able to see at first hand the progress and sense of achievement of some pupils with special educational needs whose class were developing new computer skills. The work and degree of support was being finely tuned to the needs of individual pupils. One boy had typed in his words without spaces. His instinct was to delete it all and start again but once he was shown how to place the cursor and use the space bar, he was able to take pride in his work. His spontaneous comment: 'I feel good'. He decided to print two copies, one for his classroom and one to take home. He was delighted to hear his sentences read aloud by the *Scriptit* software.

Individual talents and needs are catered for. The special needs assistant stressed the importance of fostering individual talents, as you would in a family. In her role, she often saw how pupils with literacy problems would shine in art or modelling or were the best actors.

Shortly afterwards, I met six Year 5 pupils who were members of the Advanced Maths Group – normally taught by the head Pam Matty during the numeracy hour as a mixed-age class from years 4-6. The Year 6 pupils were invited, if they wished, to sit the GCSE, and most achieved B or C grades at the age of 11. I'd thought I was quite sharp mathematically but they ran rings round me.

They showed me how they worked on inputs and outputs, using a function. One pupil suggested *n squared plus 3*, and invited me to propose an input. I gave them 10, the immediate answer was 103. Someone else suggested *n cubed plus 3*. I cautiously gave them 2 for the input, the immediate reply 11 – too easy, they felt. So I suggested each one of them should set a question for the others to solve. Every time, I was beaten on time and often on accuracy by others in the group:

n squared plus half n, divided by 2, minus 4. Input 4.

n cubed plus n times 3, then divide by 2. Input 2.

The next one started with 'Twice n squared'. There was serious disagreement over the answer, due to the ambiguity – some had squared *2n*. I explained the standard order for processing such statements and how brackets could alter it. Immediate understanding, so others began to use this form: *2n, in brackets, squared, add 8, and divide by 9.* Some calculators came out.

Feeling this wasn't enough of a challenge, they explained that more fun was to be had if someone gave a set of inputs and outputs and you had to guess the formula. To help, they would give its general shape, using question marks of different sizes to represent the numbers, powers and signs. To tease the mathematicians reading this book, I present the problem they suggested:

input	output
0	*1.5*
7	*38.5*
5	*20.25*
3	*8.25*
1	*4.5*

Gradually, the pupil setting the problem gave out a few clues, but all the group were enjoying the challenge.

I was shown a range of other work: the magic mixer, an 'identity parade' problem, various forms of graphs, a question about which type of average was most useful in analysing some attendance data.

Some of these pupils were also in the Advanced Literacy Group. On Mondays, they had a philosophy lesson, taught by the former headteacher. Here they would be challenged to provide evidence to support their arguments, to examine the meaning of concepts they took for granted. On other days, their writing skills were being stretched – but again it was fun. The display showed a basic but rather boring sentence which they each had to transform, with ingenious variety of narrative, genre, atmosphere, characterisation.

Conclusion

The ethos of Grove Primary School is difficult to sum up. The children are courteous with one another but warm and lively. They are conscientious in their work but playful and ingenious. They concentrate well but are not expected to be sitting concentrating all day long – there is great variety of activities, appealing to many different learning styles.

There is enormous strength of teamwork, a pool of talents working together to foster the luxuriant talents of the children. The staff are energetic and mutually supportive. Development is often planned and supported by the Senior Management, but driven by the motivation of team members working together.

The curriculum is multicultural, responding to a wide range of traditions from Asia, Africa and the Americas. The teachers also believe in the entitlement of inner-city children to enjoy the Royal Ballet, impressionist painting, philosophical debate, the English countryside. It is also an antiracist curriculum, in which children of all backgrounds are encouraged to reach for the sky. Achievement is a coat of many colours, and only a small part of it can be weighed and measured.

With particular thanks to Pamela Matty (Headteacher) and Julie Reeves (SEN)

Falinge Park High School, Rochdale

Falinge Park School has had a remarkable history, after a less than promising start in life. The current school was formally established ten years ago during an authority-wide reorganisation as an 11-16 mixed comprehensive school, ostensibly serving a balanced catchment area. A new headteacher and many new staff were appointed. However, its initial character was marked two years earlier, when a 13-18 school on the Falinge site was merged with a 13-16 school in the town centre. Both were troubled schools: in one, communications had broken down between the staff and the head; the other, a temporary overflow school for the new Asian community, could boast an innovative multicultural curriculum but produced desperately low exam results. Not surprisingly, choosy parents were desperate to avoid Falinge Park. According to Glynis Foster, who has loyally served the school as Chair of Governors since its foundation:

> We were snubbed by local families. Truancy was running at 40 per cent. Only four per cent obtained five or more A-C grades, and most students left with no qualifications at all.

Last year, 27 per cent of students achieved five or more A*-C grades and 93 per cent gained five or more GCSEs. Every single student left with at least one GCSE. This was in spite of extremely high free meal levels and student mobility – a quarter of last year's GCSE candidates entered the school part way through. Sixty per cent of the students are of Asian heritage, and include a Bangladeshi community which is significantly disadvantaged in terms of overcrowded housing and parental illiteracy. Student numbers have increased by a hundred over the past year, to 934, and the lowest year is almost full. The head, Linda Woolley, is proud to boast that students now come from Norden and Bamford (one of Rochdale's most affluent areas, and nearer to another school with superior facilitites and its own sixth form!) 'We're moving rapidly towards a proper comprehensive mix, and moving up to national average results!'

Last year, OFSTED ordered a full inspection only three years after the last – a dangerous and nerve-racking event, normally triggered by suspected low standards. The school came out with flying colours and was listed by the Chief Inspector as 'an outstanding school'. It is expecting to be designated a Beacon School in the near future, with responsibilities to provide guidance and support to other schools in the region.

Extracurricular activities

Many schools will argue that it is impossible to develop after-school activities in a multicultural school, and particularly with Muslim communities. Falinge Park has won Education Extra's National Certificate of Distinction five years running. The provision has been built upon a commitment to equality of opportunity. The school has chosen to provide instrumental tuition free of charge. It has successfully entered students in the Rochdale Festival of Arts and Music, winning prizes in the public speaking events (once a white-only preserve).

The enthusiasm of staff has led to a richness of experience which few state schools can match.

- Sport – clubs include badminton, basketball, dance, football, PE, girls' football, gymnastics, lacrosse, netball, trampolining and volleyball; there are cricket and football teams; cross-country running, orienteering, a 'come-and-try-it' event, roller hockey and a Saturday soccer school.

- Subject-related visits – the French exchange, a Media Studies trip to Bradford's Museum of Film, Photography and Television, a Geography field trip to Malham, the Year 7 History visit to Roman Chester, the IT visit to Granada Studios, and so on.

- Opportunities for further study and to raise standards, including the summer literacy and numeracy schools, the education authority's Music School, computer suites open after school, and many revision lessons after school and in the Easter holidays.

- Charitable and public-service activities, such as fundraising for the NSPCC, the Mersey Basin conservation volunteer weekend, the National School Grounds Day, the North West in Bloom awards.

- An after-school club for 11-14 year olds, which would include games and activities as well as study facilities, funded by Education Extra.

Good social and leisure facilities are provided at lunchtimes in year bases and gardens (one of them accommodating the Education Extra prize of a giant chess set).

The support of parents has been won by reassuring them that their children are in safe hands. After a theatre trip, for example, Asian students are delivered to the door and handed over to their families. The parents come out, shake hands, invite the teachers in, though this has to be declined in order to get the others home. Parents who hadn't wanted to allow their children in to use the school library over the Easter holiday were contacted and persuaded to do so.

Convincing the parents – developing the school ethos

Headteacher Linda Woolley explained how these two processes have gone hand in hand at Falinge Park:

> It's a myth that parents don't care about their children's education. They do, but often they don't know how to engage with it. We have had to take the initiative, and make extra efforts to be accessible. If a parent phones, we always put them through to somebody, even if it's not the first person they asked to speak to. We send out lots of newsletters, and we communicate through the newspapers to our parents. We've been approachable when parents have complained. There've been a lot of home visits. We've shown we care about attendance. There was once a time when Year 9 boys just used to drop out of school, but not now.

> We've worked with other agencies to run family literacy projects. We've persuaded the community centre to put on workshops to help parents help their children. We've recently been talking about targeting 20 year olds, older brothers and sisters who were once our students, and are therefore often better placed than their parents to help the current students.

The trust has been built up over many years. Parents know that we do not tolerate violence or racism here, the bottom line is respect. Going back to the time of the Gulf War, when there was a lot of tension, the sensitivity of our humanities teachers stood us in good stead, and even the most fervent Muslims said, 'We feel OK when we're inside these grounds'.

We don't tolerate a macho street culture. We've established a pride in the school. At one time we might have regarded school uniforms as reactionary, but it's been part of the pride, an '*in your face*' response to the old reputation of the school and to the negative aspects of the street culture.

That hasn't meant cutting ourselves off from the real world. In fact, our school values are very close to the values of the home, and particularly the Asian communities. We draw on that kinship-based value system: 'You've upset someone in my family'. Our set of values is really very simple: *respect, family* and *achievement.*

We expect and get honesty when things go wrong. Our students hold their hands up, 'Yes, I did wrong, I'm sorry.'

We felt the support of parents when the OFSTED inspectors came – parents were sending us chocolates and flowers. The parents know how hard we work.

This depends on a commitment from all the staff – they all accept a strong pastoral role, and there is a very proactive tutor system.

Repeatedly during my visit, teachers and students confirmed this perspective. Students expressed gratitude for how ready their teachers were to provide individual help. A teacher explained that parents, after listening to accounts of the student's progress, would always ask, 'Is he well behaved?' 'This is *izzat* – the family honour is at stake, and they are grateful for our positive response'.

The Chair of Governors praised the head's leadership and the commitment of the whole staff:

Teachers have given over and above anything we could reasonably expect of them.

We've taken great care with staff recruitment. Interviews have been rigorous and lengthy – we've had to know that new teachers were on the same wavelength, that they had a good understanding of equal opportunities issues, that they were willing to engage in extra-curricular activities.

The year tutors have played a crucial role. We don't let our students reach a stage when they feel they can't catch up.

Another fast-improving local school had set up a 'target group' to help it make an initial breakthrough, to show that some students could achieve examination success. We chose not to go down that road, which in some ways was harder, but we've always been firm on inclusiveness. They all know they can achieve something, even if they're not achieving A*-C grades. We have worked very hard on their study skills, shown them how to achieve, used assemblies to stress achievement. Most of our students believe in achieving their *personal best*. We've tended towards mixed ability classes rather than setting, though there is flexibility. (Glynis Foster)

It's obviously an additional burden on staff time when students arrive from other schools, and teachers spend a lot of time with such newcomers, but the commitment of the vast majority of students is essential here, in providing a positive environment. 'Our students won't take nonsense, and we've had some real successes with students who've had to leave other schools'.

It's understood that Beacon School status will mean a good deal of extra work, but the challenge is being taken on also with an eye to the school's public status and what it will mean to the parents.

Quality and development

The head and deputies have succeeded in combining powerful leadership with active collegiality. A large part of this comes from working to ensure agreement of principles among the staff. It is understood, for example, that all staff are pastoral and that the school needs a proactive tutor system. Initially, PSE was taught through separate lessons and with specialist staff. The tutor time was extended to include more PSE, while retaining a weekly lesson by specialists, but now agreement has been reached to switch to a one-hour lesson per week run by the form tutors. The head says, 'I keep asking 'Are we ready? Are you sure?''

Monitoring of lessons was built up gradually over several years and its success depends on teachers understanding its value. It began with monitoring homework and was directed at certain points in the student's career rather than specifically at the teacher. Normally now, the teacher being monitored has the choice of focus, but in the absence of more specific priorities, the key areas are *equal opportunities* and *removing barriers to learning*. The head gave me the example of her monitoring visit to look at students' participation. As an observer, she noticed that a little group of quiet Bengali girls were sitting on the periphery of the teacher's vision and were not fully included in the whole class activity. The teacher was able to make use of this information, and began giving these girls extra attention during group activities. Monitoring is not just a top-down activity, and heads of faculty are encouraged to delegate this role to others.

One of the ongoing obstacles to school development is the short-term nature of funding initiatives. Language Support teams have been run for over ten years on this basis, and many talented teachers have moved out of them into mainstream posts as a result. During my visit, a good deal of the head's time was taken up with personnel work connected with placing these teachers on the school's payroll. It was not an even playing-field – the funding allocation was cut, meaning a reduction of 2.5 teaching staff and, even so, the grant was only guaranteed for two years. The new Social Inclusion grant was being given out for a year at a time – hardly the basis for professional management and school development.

Similarly, this school, like many others, has been penalised by the way in which school budgets are allocated. These are based on a form completed in January – the most popular time for extended visits to Pakistan or Bangladesh. Students transferring late to the school have to be carried cost-free for up to a year, and yet these are students who cause so much extra work. The school expects to receive asylum seekers but is given no precise information about funding. Clearly, the standard budgetary arrangements are better suited to schools with a settled population, whereas many inner city schools, especially those with some spare spaces, receive many students as the result of their failure to settle in other schools, family breakup, and parents who move to seek work or flee debt.

A firm foundation: Year 7

The National Curriculum in England was designed as a number of discrete subjects, on the assumption that each would be 'delivered' by its own specialists. In many schools, this halted a trend towards greater integration in the lower secondary years and stability for students following transfer from primary school.

Falinge Park has opted for a more integrated approach in Year 7. A foundation programme covering English, Geography, History and PSE is taught by the form tutor, who is in contact with the class for over 40 per cent of the time. There is a single Science teacher, and a carousel arrangement for technologies and arts. So there is considerable stability for new students.

The Year 7 classes are taught the foundation programme in their own classrooms, grouped together in a single block with its own dining room and other facilities. The students evidently felt at ease, as I saw for myself when students drifted back to their form room at the end of the morning session.

This also made the class teacher more sensitive towards individual personalities and learning needs and better placed to give advice and help. One teacher spoke of her greater awareness of students' preferred learning styles. An example was given of a dyslexic student who preferred pictorial forms of note-taking and used this method effectively to give a confident talk to the class.

The Year 7 teachers work closely as a team, on pastoral and academic levels. The team included some experienced and senior staff as well as newly qualified teachers. They are able to draw on their particular academic backgrounds while focusing substantially on literacy and learning skills.

The daily half-hour tutor time includes individual preparation for the Spelling Challenge, with certificates given to those reaching targets, and paired reading helped by Year 10 students. There is plenty of spoken language, for different subjects. Each classroom has its own bookbox. Frames have been designed to structure reading and thinking and to teach academic syntax. (For example, a frame to support the study of Roman artefacts and architecture had the column headings, 'We can see that... This tells us that... I think the Romans had/ used/built .... to ....')

Students become conscious of their own learning and gain status from it. They share their work, read it out aloud. A folder is kept of key pieces of work, right up until the end of Year 9. Periodically, the file is examined and students evaluate the progress they have made, but they also show each other, with evident pride.

The coherence of the Foundation Programme means that the teacher can develop in a planned way the different genres of writing appropriate to different subjects and purposes. An Independent Learning Day had taken place in the previous week, to develop skills of information seeking.

Various teachers spoke of the culture developed in year 7, of friendship, of the more able helping others, of ensuring that everyone has understood, of valuing different cultures, of mutual respect, of being willing to learn from others. I saw a student approach his class teacher because he was concerned that another student had fallen out with him. This was a safe environment, with secure and trusting relationships. One Year 7 class had produced an assembly for their Year and were asked if they'd be prepared to do it for others. They agreed to put it on for Years 8 and 9 – a good indicator of self-confidence for students who had only been at the school six months.

One deputy head summed up this 'mini-school' idea as *Team, Territory and Time*. An HMI had advised them, 'If you get Year 7 right, the rest will follow.' It had helped to establish a learning culture in the school and had given it a particular appeal to parents.

The inspection teams had focused attention on this arrangement, and concluded that the students were making more progress in six months than Year 7 students normally achieve in a year, without the regression that usually follows transfer.

A curriculum is for learners

Many schools have felt constrained by the National Curriculum, despite being critical of its Eurocentrism. The head explained how careful departments had been to seek the best opportunities within it, for example through careful choice of GCSE board for a particular subject, such as an art syllabus which offered more flexibility of materials, including textiles. A GCSE Humanities course dealing with live issues of prejudice, war, famine, persecution etc. was a popular choice, alongside history, geography and RE. The English department had developed students' love for Shakespeare by their choice and treatment of the plays for study. 'Equal opportunities runs through all our work – it's about personal effectiveness and removing barriers to learning.' In the mathematics rooms, I found posters about the Islamic origins of algebra, and how numbers are written down in different cultures and languages.

The displays in the main corridor all spoke to me about a curriculum concerned with real people and real concerns, which frequently connected with students' perspectives and experience:

- Geography: Bangladesh, the good and bad points about Majorca

- History: immigration, war, the Holocaust, women at war, the home front; historical events presented as contemporary newspapers (the 'Canterbury Times' with its headline 'Knights went nobbling...' told of the murder of the archbishop for opposing the king

- Creative arts: Asian and African dance

- Religious education: spiritual values, ultimate questions, the sacred symbols of different religions

- Bengali, French, German and Urdu: displays reflecting students' interests, the environment

- Humanities: culture and belief, equality and injustice, persecution, conservation.

During the course of three successive lessons, I was able to see examples of this serious engagement and connectedness with students' lives and experiences.

History – digging into experience
The Second World War predates the arrival of most Asian communities into Britain and yet it is a significant event for modern Britain and the world. I would argue that it has a rightful place in the core curriculum, and question any version of 'multiculturalism' which wanted to remove it. It was interesting to see how it was taught at Falinge Park.

Making it more relevant included looking at the role and treatment of soldiers from the Empire, but this is probably not the central issue. The two most important issues were clearly antisemitism and total war. One History teacher reminded his class of their GCSE assignment, a diary of life as a Jew in Hitler's Germany, due in the next week, and the theme was emphasised through wall displays. Most of the lesson I saw was about the concept and experience of 'total war' – central to understanding our world today.

Gradually, building upon factual knowledge from a previous year, the class worked towards coherent understanding. The central concepts were written on the blackboard, to help focus discussion rather than as words to learn. Some questions were for recall of earlier learning, but they were driven predominantly by the need to link these separate pieces of knowledge together to provide a framework for wider understanding.

> T: It's often called *total war*. [writes on board] What does that mean, do you think?
>
> P: All wars added up.
>
> P: Maybe about all countries joining in...
>
> T: Maybe. Any other ideas?
>
> P: Everybody has to take part in the war.
>
> T: Can you explain?
>
> P: Like women have to make ammunition.
>
> T: So we have there an example...
>
> P: A big war.
>
> P: An official war.
>
> T: What would you mean by an unofficial war?
>
> P: Like Northern Ireland. Not in uniform...

The discussion is clearly exploratory. The teacher is careful not to undermine these tentative contributions, but steers, replaces, shifts.

> T: Some people would say the First World War was not a total war. Who didn't get involved?

P: Old people.

P: Women.

P: Some did. They made weapons.

P: They brought up their families.

T: But they didn't have to, did they? ... So in a total war, everybody gets involved, everybody has to be involved. [gradually building up the idea on the blackboard]

Students are invited to see it through civilian eyes, in their own terms.

T: Where do you live?

P: South Street. [right at the centre of Rochdale's Bangladeshi community]

T: In the First World War, you'd be safe in South Street. There weren't many bombers, just balloons, mainly on the south coast of England. What about the Second World War? How did it begin?

P: A blitzkrieg.... lightning war... bombers...

Students remember facts from their previous year's course: gas masks, blackout curtains, Anderson shelters, legs stained with gravy browning to look like nylon stockings. Constantly, it is linked back to their immediate experience:

T: Has anybody been in a plane at night?...

T: Why might life be hard for a housewife in the kitchen?

T: What were factories around Rochdale making during the war?

The teacher tells them how his mother made a dress from a damaged parachute:

How many of you would make your own clothes? If you travelled back in time, I bet you'd be trying to find a sports shop to buy something with a designer label.

The session moves on from whole-class work to collaborative reading in groups of a passage about the 'Kitchen Front' – a supportive form of independent learning for the students in this mixed-ability class whose English was less secure.

Antiracist English and media studies

An English class were finishing off work towards their GCSE folios and this provided a good opportunity to see the type of work being done. One wall display included newspaper reports reflecting the racial conflict in the American Deep South, following a reading of *Let the Circle be Unbroken* (a 'prequel' to *Roll of Thunder, Hear my Cry* by Mildred Taylor.) The *Mississippi News* demanded the hanging of blacks for damaging the wagon of a white racist farmer, 'Them niggers have gone too far'. *The Mississippi Black Times* announced, 'White boys stir up trouble', 'Blacks need justice'. The stockroom included a wide selection of multicultural novels. Good use was made of the NEAB poetry anthology, with its emphasis on diversity.

The chosen Shakespeare text was *The Merchant of Venice* and its treatment was interesting. This is traditionally read one-sidedly as an antisemitic text but here the students had clearly been able to follow the detail of Shakespeare's exploration of cultural and ethnic hatred and see how he exposed the treatment of Shylock by the Venetian elite. Their writing pointed up Antonio's hypocrisy for borrowing money from a man he hates, the gentiles' mocking complicity when their servant elopes with Jessica, their devious use of the law and ruthless pursuit of revenge, alongside the damage to himself and others of Shylock's bitter anger. The students are better able than most literary critics to understand emotions and reactions not as individual emotional outbursts by 'characters' but as part of a cultural context, with its structure of feeling built upon racism and unequal power.

The piece of writing being handed in concerns the treatment of Muslims in the press and on television. Two 'texts' have been studied, Carol Sarler's opinion column in *The People* (Sept 28 1997), and an episode of 'Casualty'.

Carol Sarler, describing herself as 'Britain's sassiest columnist', begins her invective: 'It's time we stood up to these Muslim bullies'. She ends with the warning: 'If we don't stand up to it soon, in 50 years time it won't be beheadings in Riyadh we have to worry about. *It will be beheadings in Ruislip*' (her italics).

The incitement to hatred is 'supported' by miscellaneous and extreme 'evidence', roaming between 'death threats to those who write books that some happen not to enjoy', 'enforced rape of those little girls in what is laughingly called an arranged marriage', and the 'slow and cruel slaughter of animals according to Islamic custom and British revulsion'.

Students make the most of this opportunity to analyse the rhetorical devices, and reach a mature understanding of how language is used to manipulate and to assert power:

The word 'we' is used to divide the Muslims (black) and Christians (white). Carol Sarler assumes that all the readers are not Muslims and that they feel the same way as she does...

Then she says 'these Muslims' assuming that all us Muslims are bullies...

Carol Sarler uses many linguistic devices such as alliteration, repetition and exaggeration. She uses phrases such as 'Muslim menace' or 'Islamic nutters' which are pejorative... She goes on to say, 'They are laughing at us, thrilled with their power, revelling in their barbarity'. What she's saying is that we Muslims are inhuman. She's saying that we are barbarous and not civilised human beings...

Then she says 'rabid rabbles', as supposing we are dogs with rabies and disease. Yet again she is skilfully adding words that don't need to be said....

She next attacks mosques which are 'preaching the annihilation of infidels'. What on earth is she talking about? I don't know about her but what I was taught in mosque was the complete opposite. She's got very strange thoughts running around in that brain of hers which are really disturbing. I wish I could show her exactly what they teach in mosques then maybe she'll get her facts right next time before she writes such a whole lot of fabrications.

It's true that girls get arranged marriages, but rape? Where did she get this idea from? From my sister's arranged marriage, I saw that my brother-in-law and sister kept in contact, learnt about each other, and accepted each other. Just because it's an arranged marriage doesn't mean the girl gets raped and anyway arranged marriage is not in our religion but in our traditional culture. It's a bit like instead of going out clubbing looking for someone, your parent looks for you, making sure they come from a good family and background...

> She takes extreme accusations and presents them as if they're normal things that happen in every Muslim family...

The work on 'Casualty' represents a similar sharpness of analysis. The students raise questions about balance and misrepresentation, asking why positive experiences of arranged marriages, or indeed any happy experiences of family life, never appear on television.

They are able to understand how television uses its own rhetorical devices to manipulate meanings.

> Then comes the part when Lamisha and Damien, who are in love, are going to get caught by her brother and his friend. As they are being chased off, Khalid the big brother strides in through the dark iron gates and stands there with his cigarette in his hands taking a long puff at it. His eyes looked big and round with that look of cool anger burning up inside them. You can tell this instantly that he's the bad guy right from the start, even before he could say a word. His partner or friend, before he opened the gate, made it look as though it was a jail or a cage...

> He strides in from darkness to light. This atmosphere was very threatening and menacing. He's got shadows cast upon his face, illuminating and menacing. We as the viewers are manipulated straight away that this Asian big brother Khalid is the bad guy...

> The only lights in the tunnel were supplied by the car headlights, and even then there were shadows cast everywhere in the dark tunnel...

> These two characters are dehumanised and are not presented as full human beings. Their clothes gave them a stiff rigid look as they walked towards them... They looked like silhouettes, with no emotion, and their dark shadows had dark colours around them such as black, brown, grey, showing no sign of life or joy...

The students question the villains' use of an ambulance to run down their sister's boyfriend. 'The scriptwriter could have used their black car instead, but they show that an ambulance, which is meant to save lives, as soon as it's got into an Asian person's hands, it's turned into a killing machine or a weapon of death.' Charlie's and Baz's wedding provide an immediate stark contrast to this other love story. The students point out that all the scenes involving the Asians are shown in darkness, even though the interspersing shots of the hospital and the wedding indicate that they take place in broad daylight.

Their conclusions point to the imbalance and racism of media representations of Muslim Asians in particular, and the danger this represents.

This engaged form of English teaching not only provides a site for students to explore issues of identity, culture and power through language, it has also delivered results in crude examination terms. Despite the weakness of many students' English when entering the school, 99 per cent gained a GCSE in English, including nearly 40 per cent at grades A*-C. All the students were also entered for English literature, with 97 per cent passes, and nearly 50 per cent A*-C grades. The media studies option is increasingly popular and very successful.

The Media Studies class were building on the study of the 'Casualty' episode and looking at the representation of Asian people in other popular forms, including documentary and feature film. The issues relating to representations, balance and rhetorical effects were being studied, with a close eye to issues of light, sound, camera use, commentary. The rare examples (e.g. 'A suitable girl') of work by Asian documentary production teams were examined. Obsessions and omissions were discovered:

> Has the theme of arranged marriage become an obsession for the media?

> Why are there no accounts of Asian girls going into careers? Or if it's shown, they're totally westernised?

Altogether, students concluded that Muslim Asians in particular were under-represented and misrepresented, that there was negativism and alarmism, and a failure to understand or to consult with Asian communities in Britain.

Conclusion

The teachers at Falinge Park have achieved success in an extremely difficult context. Morale is often low in the town, where no new industries have emerged on any scale to replace the cotton mills which first attracted immigration from Pakistan. One of the consequences of this economic disappointment is the degree of isolation of the Muslim communities from other parts of the population.

It is an enormous tribute to the school that such high morale has been built there, along with a curriculum which helps these students make sense of their world.

With particular thanks to Linda Woolley (Headteacher), Glynis Foster (Chair of Governors), Robin Lonsdale (Deputy Head and History), George Wikowski and Mark Howell (English and Media Studies).

Dalry Primary School, Edinburgh

For most people across the world, Edinburgh means the tourist attractions – the Castle, Princes Street, the military Tattoo. As a tourist centre, it sells itself through the icons of nationhood – bagpipers playing in front of the big stores. Each year, thousands of visitors arrive for the International Festival but few visitors realise just how international this city now is.

Dalry Primary School is situated only a mile away from the castle. Almost all its children live in small Victorian tenement flats. (In Dalry, typically four storeys high, with eight flats leading from a central stair, repeated along a terraced street or the main road.) Many of the buildings are now falling into disrepair. Apart from the clothes-drying green at the back of each block, there is nowhere to play in the area but the school playground. The school's catchment area is sandwiched between a railway line and a busy dual carriageway. Around 60 per cent of the pupils have free dinners.

About 20 per cent of the children are bilingual, from a variety of different backgrounds including Indian, Pakistani, Bangladeshi, Chinese, Egyptian, Nigerian. Until the school began to develop a multicultural and community ethos, many were suffering serious isolation.

The school has Positive Discrimination status, giving it a better pupil-teacher ratio. It is taking part in Scotland's national literacy initiative, Early Intervention, which is more loosely framed than England's National Literacy Strategy but has some characteristics in common. Thanks to a variety of initiatives, including greater clarity about expectations, a transformation of the school environment, parental involvement initiatives and the high morale of staff and pupils, there is a high quality to the learning and achievement is improving significantly.

Rebuilding a community

David Fleming, headteacher for the past five years, sees his role to be as much about rebuilding the community as developing its school. Indeed, the two cannot rightly be separated.

> You can't deal with issues just inside the school. There are no parks in this area. The housing is jammed between a dual carriage and a railway line. The school playground is the only space. So it's vital to the children's growth and well-being that we improve that space and make it safe. That's why we've spent time bidding for funds to build equipment. We've planted flowers. We've put in security cameras and floodlighting to make it safe on the dark winter evenings.

> I think we've got to consider these children's experience very carefully. We're only two miles from the Royal Botanic Gardens, but even some people who've lived here many years haven't heard of them, and they never get out into the countryside. There's no use talking of sheep and cereal crops in our lessons if children haven't seen these things.

> We try our best to compensate. The Volunteer Tutors Organisation take children and families on excursions to other parts of the city. After the education cuts of several years ago, we no longer have the funds for excursions. The four-day school camp is a very important experience, but that costs £175, which is too much for some families. This used to be cheaper before the Regional Council was broken up.

The head is active in the Community Council and has used it as an aid to networking and developing new projects for the school and the area. A number of groups now use the school, including NKS (Nari Kalyan Shango), an Asian women's group running a class for mothers to help overcome isolation. The school works closely with the Health Board and Social Services.

> No one really takes an overview of community needs, so we have to network with many different organisations. We use the Bilingual Health Project to provide a keep-fit class. We use Council funding for adult education so that we can host an Urdu class. And we run many events ourselves, including celebrating the religious festivals.

The head frequently uses the word 'clan'. It is a symbol of the extended family and of neighbourliness, rolled into one. It signifies a common culture, an acceptance of responsibility for others. At a symbolic level, it connects with Scottish rural tradition, with working-class urban solidarity and with the Asian extended family. All of these connections occur when he is declaring the values which drive the school.

> This may be myth, but it could be an important myth to hold onto and take us forward. We need an alternative vision to those normally offered us. If all we've got is the media version of social responsibility – the adverts for children to stuff themselves with crisps to save tokens for school books – then we're not going to move forward very positively.

Finding a place and a voice
The head is well aware of the isolation felt by many ethnic minority families in the area. Some have experienced harassment, and he has personally accompanied them to meetings with the housing associations, applying pressure to get them into a flat where they feel more secure. Some families will not go out on a Saturday when there is a football match at the nearby ground.

The appointment of three bilingual staff in the last few years has marked a sea change. One came to the school in 1997; she works on the Early Intervention (i.e. literacy and numeracy) programme with Primary One and manages the parents' room. There is also a classroom assistant and a special needs auxiliary. In reality their roles are flexible and to some extent self-created. As the classroom assistant explained, 'I used to work as special needs auxiliary, mainly on a one to one basis. Now I am assisting teachers in various classes but also interpreting on parents' evenings and liaising with parents on other occasions. I arranged a play for Diwali and took pupils to the Hindu temple.'

They have brought with them a variety of experience and qualifications: work in a children's centre, an RSA diploma in teaching community languages, research in community education. They speak and understand an unusual range of languages, particularly Bengali, Panjabi, and Hindi/Urdu, and one also has some Chinese and Arabic! Their greatest asset may be their intercultural skill, their ability to mediate between home and school cultures and to develop an active partnership in education.

At the weekly bilingual coffee morning, mums talk of their experiences and their problems. They are overcoming isolation and discovering a voice. The sessions often include keep-fit classes and craft workshops.

Eid and Diwali are celebrated. The bilingual staff must have emptied their wardrobes to provide saris for the teachers. This year, there was dancing and a short play. Eid used to be celebrated by a few Asian parents, but has grown into a major school event. Many parents provide food for these celebrations.

The parents' room has become a pleasant meeting place, decorated with Asian and Scottish images. There is a display of kilts, saris and shalwar-kamiz, and many photographs of recent events.

This provides a base for a variety of support and helps parents find their way to local opportunities which are organisationally diverse. Some mothers were advised to join the 'Number Group' at a nearby community arts centre. Others were helped to understand that the maths the school was teaching wasn't so different from what they had learnt at school in Pakistan. Some attend Urdu or Bengali lessons. Parenting classes have been organised and these were very popular. The EWO has adopted a more proactive role, running a weekly advice session: 'Is you child having any problems attending school?' says the poster. 'Are there any family problems you would like to discuss?' The keep-fit class is popular, and for many Asian mothers provides their only chance to exercise.

The mothers were often shy at first but are increasingly contributing to the children's education. Children's attitudes have changed too, as the bilingual assistants encourage them to speak in the family language. Now, local Scottish children are keen to show the bilingual staff, 'Here's something from India...I've found a picture of your country.'

The bilingual staff speak eloquently from their own experience of the children's needs:

> You have to encourage them to be proud...Teachers in some schools seem to regard children from other cultures as an inconvenience. They'll say, 'What's the point in celebrating Divali when there are only

two of them'. It's even more important if there are only two of them
– for them, and for the others. You can't just sweep our children and
our cultures under the rug.

They are aware of the cultural misunderstandings that can arise,
which can hinder the partnership between home and school. One
mother was most upset that her children were playing with water and
other materials in the nursery. She had expected them to be formally
taught the alphabet, because they were at school. The bilingual staff
were able to explain the misunderstanding to the teacher and to explain to the mother that this was purposeful play – children needed
to learn colours and shapes, to develop concepts and vocabulary for
heavy and light, full and empty. 'We should explain the purpose of
nursery education from the start, rather than assuming a shared
understanding.' Increasingly, mothers feel confident that their own
knowledge of clothes and food fits into the primary curriculum.

A learning environment

The school is operating against a background of under-investment
and lack of understanding of children's needs. The specialist EAL
teacher visits only for a few hours a week. There is no clear entitlement for the Chinese girl in Primary One who has just arrived with
no English, or for the boy in the same class who has just returned
from an extended stay in Pakistan. The bilingual assistant provides
substantial help, but more is needed.

The head has had to make difficult choices in order to turn the
school round. The building was in a poor state when he took over.
Now it is a welcoming environment which stimulates learning. The
money to repaint and refurnish classrooms was found by doing
without a deputy head for three years! Good use is being made of
vacant classrooms to provide a library, a music room where children
can enjoy playing without worrying about disturbing the class next
door, an art room. Teachers are taking on new roles and developing
rapidly – two probationer teachers have taken on the responsibility
of transforming the art room.

The central hall and stairwell sets the tone. There are giant potted
plants. The stairs are lined with children's photos and their work.
There are certificates of achievement, showing various languages.

There are large banners, in Scots and English and Urdu and Bengali, saying 'Welcome tae oor skule'.

It is clearly understood that the traditional boundaries between school and community need to be broken down and that this benefits everybody. Now that extended families scarcely function among white urban families and the ethnic minority children here are often isolated from theirs, children of different backgrounds are discovering surrogate grandparents and older people are able to enjoy children's company.

New challenges in teaching and learning

Gradually, through mutual support and cooperation with bilingual staff and parents, a more positive and imaginative learning culture is being built. When the Primary One children arrive in the morning, the teacher says a warm 'Good morning' to each child before marking off the register, and many of the children reply in their home languages. After some intensive work on the alphabet, two children are proud to show me how they can write in Chinese and Urdu.

There has been a parallel transformation to that in English schools in teaching literacy, though without dictating a single pattern. Children gain confidence through reading aloud together and through structured activities in groups. The groups are carefully chosen, making good use of the available staff – the teacher, a student-teacher and the bilingual assistant, who is able to switch between Urdu and English to help the boy who's been away for several months. The teacher takes a group of more confident readers aside to tackle a new book. There is a judicious balance between individual, group and whole-class activity, but clear benefit from collaboration and sharing – achievement is now more visible and rewarding. Children are constantly invited to demonstrate their knowledge and are clearly gaining in confidence. There is also greater economy and focus to the instruction, for example in the work I saw on vital 'function words', where the teacher concentrates on non-phonetic peculiarities and highlights the more reliable letters in 'you' and 'are'.

The teacher explains the benefits of Early Intervention:

We used to take all morning to hear everybody read. We took all year to learn the letters of the alphabet. New opportunities have arisen from this different organisation, and additional staff have been crucial. We're also more conscious of individual development, and baseline testing helps us to intervene in a more focused manner and have greater satisfaction from children's progress.

In an older class, Primary Five, the teacher has developed a close personal approach which can also be firm and critical. Good use is made of the refurnished room. Children begin the session sitting alongside their teacher, in a rectangle on the seating in one corner of their large room. There are only twenty-one pupils in this class, since this is a Positive Discrimination school, so the teacher is frequently able to differentiate and monitor and intervene in individual learning.

By accident, most of the pupils are boys. There is scope to develop imagination and initiative. For Technology, the pupils are designing novel forms of transport: a vehicle to lift and transport their school building to a new site; a digger which will tunnel and fill the hole behind; an amphibious vehicle; a microscopic instrument which will travel through your arm to fix a torn heart muscle. This is not a teacher-dominated lesson, nor is the talk dominated by one-way questions. It is speculative and exploratory talk, in which pupils easily take over from the teacher, who often invites response not through direct questions but through 'so...' and 'if...' Questions are used gently to challenge pupils to think more deeply, to explain: 'But how will that work?'

In their maths lesson, there is a strong commitment to learning from all the pupils, and a high level of concentration. The pupils are keen to do their best in their forthcoming tests but know that these will be at an appropriate level and that the teacher will help those for whom language is an obstacle by reading aloud some of the questions.

It is an established pattern in this class that, before the individual and group work, all the children sit together on the corner seating to discuss the session ahead. The teacher sits alongside them on the bench and so they form a square. Children raise questions and misunderstandings. Some children have noticed they're using a textbook known to be used in the next year group, and are reassured that they will cope with and enjoy the work and that it will make them more confident learners in the future. The teacher feels it's important to give pupils an understanding of where they are going, and each day starts with a review of the pattern of activities.

The morning ends with a quiet co-operative game in which a small softball is thrown and caught around the room – another means of strengthening relationships for working together.

Conclusions

A great deal has been achieved in transforming the ethos of Dalry School in a short time, and a positive climate for learning has been established. The situation here is different from schools where there is a high concentration of bilingual pupils and the solutions cannot be the same, but similar principles apply. The bilingual assistants are absolutely right to insist on the right of every child to have home and heritage culture noticed and celebrated.

There are also particular institutional problems for this more dispersed situation. The school is visited for several hours a week by a specialist EAL teacher from the central service, mainly to provide extra individual help. There is no established tradition, however, of EAL specialists working together with the mainstream teachers and bilingual assistants, of partnership teaching to model new approaches, methods which hopefully will also benefit monolingual speakers. Thus it is no surprise that I saw relatively little talk initiated by the pupils, little structured collaborative work which will develop spoken language and serve as a basis for writing. As the head suggested, there may well be issues to be debated, such as the unconscious lingering of old traditions: that vernacular Scots had no place within school or even that children should be seen and not heard!

Scottish teachers have been fortunate to avoid some of the more authoritarian impositions of change seen in the English system. This is not to say that they don't feel acutely a pressure to improve attainment. The rhetoric is of educational breadth but evaluation is sharply focused on literacy and numeracy. Sometimes similar ideas to those in England are introduced, but under a different name, for example, the stress on identifying sentence components. Sometimes, I sensed the negative pressures resulting from the introduction of new methods without adequate training or discussion in depth, as when details of textual structure interrupted the flow of narrative and the search for meaning. ('How many words in this sentence? Can this be a sentence if it ends with an exclamation mark, not a full stop?' How important is this really for six-year-old beginner readers?) Only through professional assertiveness, through the strengthening of collegial debate and responsibility, will these limitations be overcome.

The staff I met at Dalry have made enormous headway in establishing a warm, positive ethos, which is paying off in terms of learning and progress. The pupils have a strong sense of their own worth and a mature self-discipline and enthusiastic attitude to learning. They clearly enjoy their time at a school which is becoming the focus of the local community.

With particular thanks to David Fleming (Headteacher), Sukla Roy, Kirem Duggal and Meliha Sheikh (teaching assistants), Gill Dransfield (Primary One) and Jenny Dobie (Primary Five).

Whetley Primary School, Bradford

Whetley Primary School in Bradford serves one of Britain's longest established Pakistani Muslim communities. As with other towns in West Yorkshire and Lancashire, the first generation to come from Pakistan were attracted by jobs in the textile industry, only to find it in serious decline. Unemployment is high, especially among the Asian community. Nearly 40 per cent are known to be entitled to free school meals, and many more may be. Nearly half the children in the area live in overcrowded housing.

The Asian community has always placed great hopes on education, but was often disappointed. One of the teachers told me how her generation were segregated into a special language centre and then divided up and bussed around the city. The system stirred up racism: the children had to face not only an alien environment but also the antagonism of other pupils who couldn't understand why the 'Pakis' got away with arriving late and leaving early. Attainment levels at 16 are still very low in the city. The LEA is in the process of reorganising away from a middle school system to ensure greater continuity of education. Whetley was a First School, for 5-9 year olds, but will have the complete primary age-range by next year.

The school has 440 pupils, including 80 part-timers in the nursery. Nearly all the pupils come from homes where English is not the first or main language. The Asian community here is very self-contained and most children arrive at school with little English. Even after nursery and reception classes, they are a long way from being able to cope easily with the National Curriculum. The teachers have given careful thought to providing a curriculum which meets pupils' needs, particularly in terms of language development.

Language development and literacy

Already in 1994, the staff were engaged in developing pupils' spoken language in a systematic way. Many felt that the National Curriculum was always looking for written evidence of achievement. This had the effect of marginalising spoken language but also of seeing writing as product, not process. With the help of LEA funding (the AIMS project), they were able to spend two days each, in teams, on staff development focused on oracy, thinking through theoretical and practical issues. They worked through the National Curriculum looking for opportunities to practice spoken language.

Subsequently, some teachers became interested in First Steps, initially for writing, and the language coordinators attended a First Steps trainers' course. Now they are working on reading but they are determined to pace this development properly. They have begun with lesson observations and a review of current practice.

The literacy coordinators are critical of many features of the Literacy Strategy, regarding it as a poor derivative of First Steps. They feel that in many schools it has generated superficial staff development, so that many teachers have subscribed to the contents and timing but without a deeper understanding of theory and methodology.

Similarly, for pupils, the Literacy Strategy places a heavy demand to cover new concepts and specific skills, but these are not well consolidated and the staff feel that the careful consolidation emphasised by First Steps is crucial for their bilingual pupils. They have also been involved in a European development project called DIECEC (see Green, 1999), and learnt that Scandinavian schools in particular don't believe in too much literacy teaching before the spoken language is secure.

In fact, the practices I saw at Whetley, from the nursery to Year 3, were a well-judged and thoroughly professional combination of oracy and literacy, and always rooted in experience. Letter recognition was emphasised in the nursery class during the same activity as basic spoken vocabulary was introduced; children were role-playing as a stage in learning to write a newspaper report in Year 3. Above all, the process, sequence and timing was carefully planned, with teachers making adjustments along the way, based upon informal assessment and evaluation. The teachers had not been deprofessionalised, as many tended to be through more mechanical introductions of the Literacy Hour.

Language, literacy and experience: the nursery class

On first appearances, there is nothing particularly unusual about the nursery class. Yet with time, the visitor can appreciate the special features.

The nursery has a structured play environment, which children use enthusiastically. They are more than ready to play out situations, picking up the telephone and telling you they are phoning for the police or for a helicopter. They will insert a wooden board into a mock toaster and invite you to eat it. Structured play is a valued technique for linguistic and social development in all early years settings. One of the key differences here, compared with a mainly monolingual school, is that when the shop is converted into, say, a travel agents, adults model out the roles and the language.

The staffing is quite intensive, with one adult to every ten pupils. Activities are designed to fulfil several objectives at the same time. All take great care to engage pupils in activities which will build up basic vocabulary and at the same time ensure the basic concepts for primary education (number, colour and so on, as well as letter recognition). The activities are reinforced through visual support, movement and, frequently, use of the home language. The teacher tells a simple story about a bear family, demonstrating on a felt board, all the time asking how many bears are in the house, who they are, what they do. This group of pupils (who began nursery only two months earlier) mainly produce only single word answers but do so with confidence and enthusiasm. The staff have to work harder here than in schools where English is more advanced. Demonstrating the letter W, the teacher shows Weetabix, translates water (pani), points to the window and mimes having a wash.

Like many schools in this study, there is an unusual emphasis on creative and performing arts. Although I had no time to observe this during my short visit, the OFSTED report was glowing. 'There is imaginative use of information technology and there are ample opportunities for the pupils to paint, draw, design, model and make things from a rich range of materials. Older pupils make their own books from personal photographs. The children sing robustly and are sufficiently confident to sing solo verses and jingles to the rest of the class.'

Language, literacy and experience: Year 2

In recent years, the Australian emphasis on genre has influenced English in our primary and secondary schools. First Steps (and deriving from it, the Literacy Strategy) has encouraged teachers of infants to make explicit the structures and other features of discourse. Here, the children had developed their own frames, for example *Setting, 3 Events, and Feelings*, when writing about news. Pupils were being advised to focus on their use of time words in this sort of writing, supported by a list displayed on the wall. This was not a mechanistic approach but the scaffolding gave them confidence to be independent.

The pupils were learning to take care with technical features of writing but to do so through work on a significant text, not exercises. On the previous Monday, the teacher had written up with the children her news from the weekend (an opportunity to extend their experience, as many of the children had limited variety in their own weekend events). This was printed out in large type and laminated, so that the children could improve it, correct punctuation, identify linguistic features and so on.

Preparation was beginning for another type of writing, known as 'procedures' (in this case, a set of instructions). Experience and talking had to come before writing. Working in two groups with the main class teacher and the language development teacher, the pupils mixed and baked cakes, talking through the steps and processes as they went. The occasion had been engineered by the teacher, who deliberately generated events for speaking and writing: the cake was for a '20 marble treat'. (Marbles had been given for good behaviour, and the pupils had chosen going to the cinema – actually, a video in class, with popcorn provided!)

Another form of writing was on the wall, the character self-portrait. This simple framework was capable of multiple variations: six sentences, beginning 'I am...I live...I like...I eat...I hate...I wish...' One child had written about the wolf in Red Riding Hood. (The Year 3 pupils drew on the same frame when writing about Greek myths.)

There is no 'literacy hour' on the timetable but, due to the level of professional consciousness, this meant more literacy, not less. Language and literacy permeate the day. Geography was linked to collective reading of the big book *Katie Morag and the Two Grandmothers*. Displays included lists of human features and the physical features of Struay. The children had plenty of questions when they found that I had travelled down from Scotland.

Language, literacy and experience: Year 3

The Year 3 class, taught by a bilingual teacher and student-teacher, had been working on myths and legends. They decided it was time to look at newspaper reports. A story of Nessie, written large by the teachers as a newspaper front-page, was read aloud.

In column two was an eye-witness quotation. Questions about the source of the information showed a lack of understanding on the pupils' part of the nature of the quotation. Some of the children seemed to know about reporters, but most did not.

> T: How did we know what was said?
>
> P1: Somebody might have passed it on.
>
> P2: Somebody phoned it.

Eventually more suggestions were made: 'reporters... put pictures to make a proof... a witness... you can put a witness's photo... interview'. The teachers realised it was time to delve behind the two-dimensional text, looking at the living processes which had generated it. They arranged a role-play, with one pupil playing the eye-witness and the rest of the class as reporters. The teachers prompted pupils into an appropriate discourse. Pupils pointed microphones (glue-sticks), said which newspaper they were from, and asked their questions. The 'eye-witness' quickly got into role, creating an identity for himself, a reason why he was at Loch Ness, and so on. The teachers suggested some more questions, to get a description of the monster, find out the witness's feelings, details of when the sighting had occurred and so on.

Now that the more articulate pupils had built a discourse model for the interview, it was time for everybody to have a go. They worked in pairs, as reporter and eye-witness.

The interviews were put on hold to make sure the pupils were asking the full range of questions. The reporters were reminded that information about the witness as well as the Loch Ness Monster would help to make the story convincing to newspaper readers. It was only now that pupils were ready to attempt to write their newspaper reports, in the same pairs, on sheets of paper large enough to share with others and then discuss.

The careful sequencing and timing of activities, linking literacy, oracy and experience, social development within the classroom and an understanding of social relationships in the modern world, was only possible because of the professionalism of the teachers. It could not possibly have arisen within the straitjacket framework of the Literacy Hour as officially prescribed.

Home-school liaison
A key role is played by the home-school liaison teacher. He co-teaches with Year 2 classes during the mornings, from 9.30, leaving afternoons free for home visits and other work. His role is wide and developing. It includes:

- translating letters home

- interpreting at parents' nights

- explaining school procedures and expectations for newcomers

- acting as a mediator on issues of religious or cultural sensitivity

- helping parents understand the school's teaching methods

- showing parents how they can help their children's education at home.

There have been many barriers to overcome, including parental perceptions of education, their own experience of education in England, language and cultural misunderstandings and so on. Parents were shy initially, but now they phone and come in to discuss their children's education. Parents are becoming much more involved, and even women wearing *hijab* (often indicative of greater remoteness from Western society) are confident when they come into school.

The school invites parents to see what happens in classrooms, to see how teachers teach and what sort of work the children do. It also shows parents how household routines such as cooking can provide educational opportunities for language and maths. Parents are encouraged to teach pupils at home in the family language. They are encouraged to share books, talking with children about the pictures if their own reading in English is insufficient and asking older brothers and sisters to help.

A homework club has been set up twice a week, supported by three of the teachers. There has been positive feedback about this from parents. A monthly newsletter is published and also other publications such as a book of poems and rhyming words in various languages. As the home-school liaison teacher explained:

> This is a good staff. They are sensitive to parents and the culture. Parents don't come with suspicious feelings. They are keen to co-operate. They are very keen on education, even if sometimes they don't understand what we're doing. They've missed opportunities themselves, and will do anything to educate their children...

> There is a lot of co-operation, learning from each other's cultures. If we listen, then matters can be resolved. Some parents were against their children changing for PE, for religious reasons of modesty. They wanted the children to wear their normal clothes. The teachers felt loosely-fitting clothes made it difficult to see the children's movements. We reached a compromise by adopting tracksuits...

> We've tried to involve parents more directly in the school, and many attend assemblies led by particular classes. We sent out a survey, asking parents about their own schooling and childhood. Mothers and fathers were involved in a big art project, the Tree of Life, which parents helped to sew. Parents are conscious of the broader aims of education. (Shafiq Ahmed)

The Tree of Life: a multimedia arts project

This project has been significant in the school community's consciousness of itself. The tree symbol has been present for some years in the school's emblem. The children went to see a huge wall-hanging from Rajasthan and to look at similar symbols across a wide range of cultures.

The symbolism is powerful and wide-reaching. As some of the children explained, 'The tree is our family. It gives us water and air. It's really kind to us.' Each part has a function – no part can live without the other. It has deep roots, and reaches out.

An artist-in-residence helped the children to develop their skills and perceptions. They went out to the park to draw all sorts of trees, to study the patterns, the barks. They read books about trees, including a story of an Indian princess who campaigned to persuade her husband and the people to care for the trees. (Deborah Lee Rose: *The people who hugged the trees* (1994))

Children used batik and embroidery to produce panels for T-shirts, and eventually produced their own wallhanging.

A South Indian dance teacher was involved, and finally a number of pupils performed at the Bradford Mela, a popular outdoor summer festival. The experience is still vivid in the minds of many of the children, and the video and photographs are being used to inspire other local schools.

School development
The processes of developing teaching skills, school ethos and community links are interwoven in successful inner-city schools. Whetley is a school strongly located in its community. The headteacher, Ron Braithwaite, of African-Caribbean origin with substantial experience of inner-city schools in London, has a clear vision of local needs. He understands the Asian community's perceptions, their disappointments at opportunities lost, and the need to overcome educational disadvantage.

A majority of teaching staff are bilingual in Panjabi or Urdu – a major achievement. Bradford and Ilkley Community College has a strong tradition of educating Asian teachers and classroom assistants, and the school has been able to recruit staff following successful placements. (Teacher Yasmin Ali recalls her decision, as an 18-year-old classroom assistant, to become a teacher, and her college's positive response in immediately admitting her and her friends to the B.Ed. course while they were simultaneously studying for O-level

English and A-levels. 'We decided we didn't want to spend our lives filling paint-pots! We wanted to be teachers!')

The staff as a whole appear close to the community they serve, and Asian teachers and teaching assistants in particular provide positive role models to the pupils and their families. Educated young Asian women frequently feel compelled to move away from their home towns to avoid some of the tensions of expectations and patriarchy, but these teachers have found ways of positioning themselves within the community and achieving its respect.

The development processes are thoughtful and measured. The head and staff have kept a cool head in face of external pressures and have chosen to build upon the progress they had already made. The OFSTED inspection team had praised their work in developing spoken English and the pupils' progress in English overall by the age of nine (at that time, the age of transfer to middle schools). The school had developed good practice in supporting and using bilingualism and in working with parents; they were paying close attention to individual learning, through informal assessment; and were engaged, by 1998, in the First Steps approach. The assessment processes have been strengthened by using the BIPS and PIPS framework in Early Years and Key Stage 1, which provide a more detailed record of progress than is available from National Curriculum levels.

The language coordinators have qualified as First Steps trainers. There is a good understanding throughout the school that a deep and sustained approach to literacy is needed, which is rooted in spoken language and experience. The First Steps philosophy is to build upon the pupils' skills, rather than imposing an external and inappropriate time-scale. It emphasises consolidation and revisiting, with timing based upon professional judgements and careful assessment. The same is true for the teachers: they had developed good skills in teaching speaking and writing, and could begin to focus more on reading. But you couldn't simply jump over a stage and rush in, whatever the external pressures. The first step was an evaluation of existing strengths and weaknesses based upon observation visits by the head and the language coordinators to every class.

The school is now expanding to cover the full primary age range, as part of Bradford LEA's reorganisation. The head and governors decided to interview all new staff rather than agree to staff transfers blindly, because it was so important to find teachers who shared its philosophy.

There is a good spirit at Whetley School among the staff and the pupils. The school is rooted in local traditions and the culture of the community it serves but open in its attitudes and determination to find new opportunities and a satisfying future for its children.

With particular thanks to Ron Braithwaite (Headteacher), Yasmin Ali and Karen Westcott (Literacy Coordinators), Shafiq Ahmed (Home-School Liaison Teacher) and Sarah Hall (Arts Coordinator).

Shawlands Academy, Glasgow

Shawlands Academy is a large comprehensive school, near enough to Glasgow city centre to include the Gorbals within its catchment area, but serving a wide variety of communities. There have been many changes since the school was founded in 1894, most notably, becoming a comprehensive and receiving a large number of Asian students.

It currently has 1400 students, spread over the six years of the Scottish system, representing a broad social mixture, though 30 per cent have entitlement to free school meals. Nearly 600 are bilingual, mainly of Pakistani Muslim heritage, but with smaller numbers from Sikh and Chinese families. It is currently expecting to receive asylum seekers dispersed from Southern England.

The current head took up post in January 1999, with headship experience in another Glasgow school. 1998 had been a troubled year for the school. Asian student Imran Khan was murdered in the street, at some distance from the school but by another student who had come to Shawland only three months earlier after exclusion from another school. This was a tragedy for Imran's family and deeply disturbing for many of the students. Both Asian and white students were afraid of further violence. The school came in for much attention from the media and from the City Council. There was a full investigation and the Council was spurred to increase its work on antiracism and supporting diversity. Although no link was found between the attack and the state of the school, the head of the school resigned.

The new head Ken Goodwin was determined to develop Shawlands, both in terms of its general educational quality and attainment (by no means poor) and in the social dimension, including antiracism and the quality of provision for bilingual students.

A sense of ownership

An interim development plan had been produced which, understandably in the circumstances, began with the object of improving staff morale. It raised some central issues but somehow the initiatives didn't meet the need. The new head felt there were too many separate initiatives that needed pulling together and that some of the aims were not shared within the school community. He spent an hour with each promoted teacher, just to listen at first, and concluded that they had high regard for the students and frequently their own department but that what was missing was a sense of belonging to the whole school.

The next step was to get agreement to a structure for consultation not just with teachers and other staff but also with parents, students and community organisations. A new development plan was produced, for three years, with four interrelated themes:

• Learning and Teaching

• Raising Levels of Attainment

• Race Equality and Harmony

• Support for Staff.

Learning and Teaching came first, to emphasise its primacy, and included resource development, co-operative learning, curriculum development and bilingualism. Raising Levels of Attainment was seen to depend as much on school ethos and positive attitudes as on teaching, attendance, and homework. The school's commitment to Race Equality and Harmony was 'inextricably linked to learning and teaching, and to raising levels of attainment' (School Newsletter to parents and students, October 1999).

The Scottish system of education has retained HMI (with no parallel to OFSTED) and placed the primary responsibility for quality development on the school. The guidance, appropriately called 'How Good Is Our School?' (1996) emphasises the need to gather appropriate evidence. Consequently, questionnaires were sent out to parents and students. Realising that the students might not be entirely open to teachers in authority in the school, other adults including Asian people were involved in interviewing students about their school experience. The system of Student Councils has was strengthened, with one per year group.

Rapid progress had to be made in producing draft frameworks for equal opportunities and for race equality. These were delegated to a working party and the head, but consultation on such issues was vital. There were two whole-staff discussions, and the parents, the student councils and interested parties such as the Community Relations Council were all involved in the debate. The school has been completely 'up front' about these issues, which are raised prominently in the glossy Prospectus, the Staff Handbook and repeatedly in the monthly newsletter.

Shawlands staff have worked closely with the new Education Authority. In the era of the Strathclyde Regional Council much good work was done in the field of race equality but this was disrupted by local government reorganisation. Recently the Glasgow City Council has become active on this front again, in policy formation and funding, establishing the Glasgow Anti-Racist Alliance (GARA) and funding community-school liaison officers.

Empowering students

As a step towards student development, there was a new drive towards active involvement and responsibility. Frequently, this is linked to work in PSE.

FAB, the Forum Against Bullying, was established, consisting of carefully chosen senior students, some of whom had been victims when they were younger. They receive training from counsellors and psychologists, part of which involves an understanding of racism. Two of the senior students are always available at breaks and lunchtimes. Anti-bullying posters 'Don't delay – tell today' are displayed around the school.

On the day of my visit, a number of senior students were off to a city-wide conference 'Youth against Bigotry', organised by students at another school. This was begun by Celtic Football Club after a boy had been stabbed and killed. Although the students were in two minds about the relationship between racism and Catholic-Protestant religious bigotry, they recognised that both involved unacceptable prejudice and violence, so the students were keen to launch a common campaign.

There have been many initiatives to raise students' confidence and ambitions, for example a 'Take your daughter to work' day and Industrial Awareness events. An 'I can do anything' day for 13-14 year olds took place before they made their option choices. On International Women's Day, girls ran a workshop for women from different communities showing the resources and facilities offered by the school. There's a two-day 'Aim High in the Community' conference, for first years, with workshops led by community groups, encouraging students to get involved in local activities.

Students have increasingly been responsible for organising multicultural events, and the purpose of the events has been clarified. The Chinese New Year celebrations involved workshops on aspects of Chinese culture, including food, calligraphy and papercraft, and members of the Chinese community came into school. The Eid celebration has grown and is used as an occasion to make the whole school community better informed. Students often run assembly. Prayer rooms have been set up during Ramadan. Special workshops were held upon the 300th anniversary of the Sikh festival of Varsakhi.

At the present stage in Scotland's development, there are many issues around a sense of identity, which Asian and other bilingual and black students need to be involved in. The school had held a cross-cultural design and fashion show on an environmental theme: 'Don't Throw It – Sew It!', in which Celtic and Asian design features were prominent. PSE classes are being engaged in designing a website for use in linking with schools in other countries. Television presenter Kirsty Wark had interviewed New Yorkers and discovered they knew next to nothing about Scotland. Interestingly, the initial brainstorm, even of the Asian students, brought up mainly tourist stereotypes – haggis, Irn Bru, tartans. The next stage was to think beyond this into the realities of a multi-ethnic Scotland.

The newsletter is used to acknowledge and praise achievement of all types. In a country which doesn't play much cricket, the school team is now a source of cultural pride for Asian boys, who nearly have the monopoly. Opportunities which don't feature in the mainstream curriculum have been introduced into Activities Week at the request of students, including calligraphy and Asian cinema.

The curriculum has been expanded to enhance the status of Bengali and Urdu, which are now full alternatives from the start. To the school's delight, fifteen white students opted this year for Urdu. This is another step in helping to raise the self-esteem of the bilingual students. The Urdu teacher told me how tempting it is for westernised Asian students to look down on their parents. 'I ask them, Where do your designer clothes come from? Your parents have worked for this. You have to be proud of them, and proud of yourself' (Fatema Nizami).

The Home Economics department has changed its menu to include Chinese and Indian cooking. This was enhancing the role and status of the students, who are then in a position to advise their teachers.

The school has recently been given International School status, which will bring a million pounds of new funds over the next few years. The aims are:

- to create a centre of excellence for languages, both European and Asian

- to strengthen the international dimension of the curriculum

- to build on the school's rich ethnic diversity

- to develop education industry links on an international basis

- to establish links with schools in other countries, through visits and the internet

- to serve as a support and model for other schools.

Above all, the celebration of diversity is promoted as a gain for all the students:

We are proud of our status as a leading Scottish multicultural school. Attending such a school helps students to become enriched by developing an appreciation of other cultures and represents effective preparation for life. (School Prospectus)

These are early days, but the school is beginning to explore developments in teaching and learning styles which will increase students' active involvement. There is concern that Asian students, who are achieving average examination success in Mathematics, might be underachieving in English. The head has begun a practice of student-shadowing. At the end of one day spent shadowing a sixteen-year-old Asian boy, he praised staff for their engagement with individuals and their supportive attitudes but commented that 'there was not a great variety in lesson structure or student activity...there was little structured student-student interaction'. His guidance for the use of support staff emphasises the need to involve the support teacher fully in the lesson and at the planning stage – not to leave them on the sidelines waiting for the chance to 'support' individuals. The response is good when students have the opportunity for active involvement, as I saw in an Urdu lesson taught by a student teacher. An examination task was turned into a quiz, boys against girls, and the most knowledgeable students gained great esteem from their peers for being high achievers.

Reaching out to parents

The policy of active involvement for students is complemented by strategies for parental involvement, led by the school's Community Liaison Officer – a post funded by GARA and the City Council.

> Students and parents were lacking in confidence and motivation. My job is to find ways of involving them in decisions and giving them a greater understanding of the school.

> The school has been concerned at the low attendance by Asian parents at parents' nights. The option evening was a case in point, so we phoned up and found that many weren't aware of the event, or didn't see its importance – they just didn't know what options were.

> This led to an increase in attendance. We adjusted the time and provided transport. We've set up Information Days for different year groups. We've tried to make policies and procedures jargon-free and translated them. We provide interpreters.

> We want parents to use the school as a community resource. There've been workshops by community-based organisations, to make parents aware of the facilities available here.

It's a mistake to think they're not keen. Many parents will encourage their children to look for a career, and not just to go into the family shop. We have to help parents understand new opportunities. Parents are often afraid of school, which represents authority. That's one good reason for increasing community activities. (Farhat Ghani)

Reflective leadership

The school has a wide range of expertise, including a well-established language support team, and staff are working together more. It is particularly fortunate in having the awareness, sensitivity and ability to theorise issues of race and diversity of the head Ken Goodwin, Anwar Din (guidance teacher) and Hakim Din (assistant headteacher). The head already has experience of managing a multi-ethnic school. Hakim and Anwar Din, as well as being highly experienced teachers, had held posts under Strathclyde's antiracist initiatives in the late 1980s, and raised many interesting issues and challenges:

Nobody has looked at the assessment bank or the supporting notes for Higher Still [Scotland's new qualifications framework for 15-18 year olds]. It took ten years to sort out the Standard Grade. The gatekeepers at the exam board are probably fairly unaware of multicultural and antiracist issues but the tests are determining what is taught...

Multiculturalism is just mixing cultures, dropping names, pretty pictures. We have to do something more. We need to challenge tradition, encourage students to take up new opportunities, provide positive images – not just doctors and waiters and shopkeepers – show a range of occupations...

We use the religious festivals also to give white students a positive view of Asian culture. We have to give them a high profile. If you celebrate Christmas for two weeks, it sets up a hierarchical perspective... The Scottish Office still officially regards the family celebration of Eid as an absence...

Sometimes I wonder if our model of PSE is culturally too simplistic. We need to question what common terms like 'assertiveness' and 'negotiate' mean when our students go home. Assertiveness is a cultural phenomenon. I wonder what happens when a Chinese student, for example, starts to 'negotiate' with her parents in the way we suggest.

The draft Equal Opportunities Policy raises many important questions. Teachers are advised to monitor whether all students are encouraged to participate in all activities and to reach maximum potential. They are asked to look critically at the criteria used for assessing students' work and the comments made by teachers. They should value 'the contribution which can be brought to the classroom by the diverse cultural and social backgrounds in our school population' and think how to encourage such contributions. 'Recent research indicates that [making references to cultural background] merely with the intention of appearing inclusive can be counterproductive and is viewed by students as being patronising.'

These are still early days in the school's current stage of development but this combination of commitment and reflection, along with the desire to involve the whole school community, points to a positive future.

With particular thanks to Ken Goodwin (Headteacher), Hakim Din (Assistant Head), Fatema Nizami (Urdu), Farhat Ghani (Community Liaison Officer) and Anwar Din (Guidance).

Golden Hillock School, Birmingham

Golden Hillock is situated in Sparkhill, Birmingham and serves some of the most deprived areas of the city. At the last inspection, 65 per cent of students had an entitlement to free dinners – an extremely high proportion for a secondary school. Almost all the students come from homes where English is not the first language: 90 per cent of the children are of Pakistani or Bangladeshi heritage and the remaining ten per cent includes Yemeni and African-Caribbean as well as white children. Islam is the dominant religion in the school and area, and a large and beautiful mosque dominates the skyline of this part of the city.

The school's improvement, under the leadership of the present headteacher Thelma Probert, is very clear. The proportion of students achieving five or more A*-C grades has risen from nine to 29 per cent in four years, and most of these gained high grades in seven or more subjects, again an improvement. The school is well within the upper quartile when compared with schools with similar free meals indicators, regardless of language backgrounds. In the past two years, the staff have reduced the proportion leaving school without any GCSEs from 22 to two per cent. (This amounted to only three students – one had disappeared and the other two were in Pakistan!) According to Birmingham LEA's preferred measure, the proportion of students gaining five or more GCSEs at grades A*-E rose from 35 to 60 per cent over a four year period.

Results like this are an important indicator and of enormous value in terms of self-esteem and future opportunities for the students concerned, but they are only part of the story. There has clearly been a major shift in culture and expectations among students and staff, as well as a transformation in the quality of educational experience.

Changing staff attitudes

One deputy head, who was about to take up a headship in another school, talked to me about changing staff attitudes. There had, he felt, been an unvoiced feeling that little could be expected from 'the children of peasants' who didn't speak English. The English department were instrumental in making a breakthrough. In addition to English language and literature, the thirty most advanced students were also entered for Media Studies, which they studied partly in their own time including lunchtimes. That these students could achieve not two but three good English-related GCSEs was an eye-opener for other staff. Nearly half of the current Year 10 are sitting English Language a year early, to allow more time for Literature and Media in year 11. To take the extreme case, last year two girls decided to set a record in the number of GCSE subjects they could pass, and each achieved fifteen A*-C grades, one of them achieving ten and the other fourteen A* and A grades. 'This may not be educationally desirable in itself, but it was a remarkable achievement and has been an inspiration to others – students and staff.'

Staff with more negative or defeatist attitudes have changed their minds over the years, or become isolated. The school is becoming highly skilled at monitoring through data, but it is the nature of response and intervention which is most important. Although target sheets and action plans can become superficial, they have 'provided a system where dialogue is more likely to happen'. A mentoring system, which began as a means of building relationships, is firmly established. A staff meeting was held to highlight the needs of more difficult students, and staff were asked who got on well with particular students and might be able to influence them. 'We don't say anything or pick on anybody who doesn't want to take part but such processes tend to marginalise cynics in a staffroom.'

Every summer after GCSE exams, each teacher writes a self-evaluation, looking at value added since Key Stage 3, suggesting reasons why some did well and some badly and considering strategies for improvement. Interviews take place with Heads of Department, who produce consolidated reports and in turn meet the head and deputies. They look together at ways forward, whether in curriculum, setting arrangements, teaching and learning styles, or ethos. A similar process takes place after the mock exams, giving time to rescue problem situations. 'We talk about things. We're in it together'.

The head elaborated on the human dynamics in the development process.

When I came here, some of the things I did were unorthodox. Mission statements were very fashionable at the time. I was suspicious of them – they were often crass or just clever slogans, or went on forever, or were contradictory, so I decided not to go through the lengthy business of designing a camel by committee.

I pondered and talked informally with staff, in search of a simple motto which we could build around. It had to say *learning* (not *achievement*, because that would follow from learning) and should be for everybody (i.e. adults too). The word was definitely learning, rather than teaching, and it wasn't just as an individual activity but co-operative. We would be learning *with* each other but also *from* and *about* each other. Finally, I arrived at *Learning Together*, which we were then able to talk about in every situation, in assemblies, in the staffroom and so on.

I needed to analyse the situation. I had good deputies, who were great (four have since moved on to headships from here) and some enthusiastic but frustrated junior staff, as well as some very well led faculties. I wanted to empower them and release their energy, so I created an upward pressure by being very open in publishing information. Teachers were asked to write three things they wanted to work on most, three aspects of the school which were good or progressing, and three which they hadn't pushed ahead on. I also asked staff about the communication channels and whether they felt their voice was being heard. Some of the heads of department didn't like this but they had to know how their colleagues saw things. We said, 'This isn't a judgement but it's your colleagues' opinions and you need to recognise the situation'. We deliberately mixed up staff in cross-departmental development committees.

We were supportive to those who'd fallen by the wayside. They'd given good service, it's just that their own development hadn't been nurtured. I'd come to the conclusion that *cynics are often disillusioned idealists*. Few teachers are cynical about children. They came into the job from idealism, but became cynical about externally imposed things. You have to make that distinction – many teachers have resorted to cynicism as a form of self-defence. I remember discussing a new initiative with one older teacher in private first. I said, 'I know you don't believe in this, but don't take it away from your colleagues. Can you spell out your disagreement clearly but then leave it to others to take this forward, without a shadow cast over it, if that's what they want to do.'

In the end, it's about children. I could be very direct. The staff realised that the school could close if it didn't change; not only were the results low but my predecessor had fallen out with the Muslim community. 'We have to improve to give the children a better deal. If you can't, it will damage the children, and your colleagues' jobs and security.'

I've also done a lot of work in changing students' attitudes. It's based on praise but I always add, 'just as I'd expect of Golden Hillock students.'

Relating to the community

In bringing parents and the community back on board, there had to be changes in various dimensions. The previous head had refused to pay attention to important community concerns and this had led to conflicts which were stirred up further by the press. Under the new head, a prayer room was quickly established, a simple quiet space with a washing facility.

We applied for a 'determination' so that school assemblies no longer needed to be predominantly Christian. For a while we had a Muslim assembly alongside the main one, but there were problems, as some of the volunteers to lead them failed to turn up at the last minute. Of course we talked to the religious leaders before discontinuing this, and they saw we had tried. The previous head had apparently argued against allowing boys to wear prayer caps, on the grounds that the same boys behaved badly in school. I told them, 'I'm glad you're proud to wear it, and you mustn't disgrace it by your other behaviour.' Now I think I've achieved a level of respect and I'm very honoured to be invited to speak at the mosques. I had to listen a lot in the early days, as there was a lot of anger and people needed to voice their concerns.

Five school council representatives, Shahid, Yasser, Aysha, Shabana and Sadiqua, spoke of the transformation in relationships within the school, and with families.

We consider ourselves as one big family, and Miss Probert is the mum. We're expected to have the same standards here as at home...She says, 'Would you throw down chewing gum at home?' ...The teachers really care about us, and we can really talk to teachers if we have any problems... Our parents do come to school, and want to know what's going on... They didn't have the same chances, and they want to support us. A lot of people come in to use the building for different events.

Parental trust had been won to allow students to take part in activities, including residential ones.

My mum didn't want my sister to go on the French trip, but my teacher went to talk to them, so they agreed...My older brothers made a breakthrough by getting to go on the residential in Wales, and now the younger ones coming to the school know that they'll be able to go too...

Older brothers and sisters who have done well at this school and gone to university have made a big difference for the rest of us. My second oldest brother is becoming a lawyer, and now my brothers are thinking of becoming doctors. In my parents' day, there was more racism. We want to make them proud of us... Sometimes it's hard for our mums when we leave home, and we need to know which is the best course so that we can explain it to them. My sister got the results and my mum said, 'So when are you moving away?' Then my sister got upset, because she thought my mum actually wanted her to go!...

We're proving we can get good jobs after this school, and students who were here before come back to talk about what they're doing now.

An ethos of empowerment

The school council reps were keen to tell me how seriously students' views were listened to.

We've had the dining room redesigned. We've got vending machines, basketball hoops, and the bully boxes. School dinners have improved, after a school council working party had a discussion with the cook. The library's improved a lot, and the lifts for disabled students...In the past, we raised money, but now we're being involved in how official resources are used...*One of the good things is teachers don't get a say —* they're not allowed to speak, because it's our school council.

They had had their own discussion on school improvement, and came to the conclusion that what really mattered is *sharing ideas, feeling you belong, mutual respect, clear targets and including everybody.*

Part of learning to take greater responsibility has involved understanding the material constraints. The other deputy head has recently taken on site responsibility and is keen to give all those who use the building – students, teachers, parents, community groups – a feeling that they are stakeholders. She is open about budgets and is asking everybody to comment on the areas they use.

> There's not much vandalism but accidental damage is expensive. I asked the caretaker to come with me to talk to the assemblies. The school council now have a Site Committee, who are systematically looking at different parts of the building. They do understand, sometimes better than teachers. There are students whose dads are builders. I want them to have a good understanding of the issues, and it's paying off. Students are approaching me with ideas. I've asked them to work out plans for improving the internal design and use of the Victorian part of the building, which is protected by a conservation order. (Eileen Brown)

The school council is clearly seen as a working model of effective citizenship. The reps meet regularly with their forms. The executive meets formally with the senior management team, and some of the younger students have major responsibilities. (The current secretary is a Year 8 girl.)

Students have also been involved in helping to transform relationships. Peer mediators have received good training, and students felt they could talk to them about sensitive family problems. The ground-rules are clear, that they will always respect confidentiality unless the student is in serious danger.

The school council also have working groups on the curriculum and teaching and learning.

A curriculum for maturity

In a further interview with the deputy head, I learnt about the philosophy behind some aspects of the curriculum.

Every student leaves with a Red Cross Certificate, based on fifteen hours of training. The Red Cross have been keen to help us, because they're looking for ways to include Asian communities, and we're hoping for a youth group. There's also the Red Cross Babysitters Award, which is really important for our families, as the older children have to look after the younger ones. It supports the community for us to promote attitudes about caring and good health, and improves our care for disabled students. (Eileen Brown)

All students do at least one vocational module and many complete Part 1 of GNVQ. The modules have been carefully chosen to develop personal and cultural competence for work and for life in general. The Leisure and Tourism module, for example, involves organising a trip for younger students. Year 10 plan a Y7 trip, and Year 11 a Year 9. They have to look at safety, at activities. 'You can see the younger ones looking up to the older ones when they see them around the school, they treat them as responsible adults, which has increased their confidence and maturity.'

The vocational activities coordinator points out that some students have rarely left the immediate area, except on car trips to relatives' homes in other cities. The GNVQ requires them to plan their own travel to the city centre. It involves first-hand experience of hospitals, the airport, the city council. The Education Authority has promoted these links and helped teachers from different schools work with public bodies to provide resources. For example, the Birmingham International Airport study pack supports work in Leisure and Tourism, Business Studies, Hospitality and Catering, as well as History, Geography and IT.

The vocational courses emphasise core skills and personal responsibility. There is a lot of communication, problem solving, looking at your own learning. There's a great deal of sharing across the LEA. The students have to research information, and work on case study scenarios. The impact of GNVQ courses is reinforced by work experience, record of achievement, the school-industry Compact and industry days. Students are encouraged to come in with their own ideas on work experience and all Key Stage 4 students have a Key Skills Logbook. There is also a system of mentors, using adults with different perspectives – teachers, classroom assistants and other adults as 'learning mentors', some from the Pakistani Mentoring Partnership. The latter are paid from the Excellence in Cities budget, and students are chosen for a variety of reasons – because they are underachieving, or need support and encouragement or have behaviour problems.

I was able to see a wide range of practical skills and social understanding during a half-hour visit to the Leisure and Tourism class: knowledge of sites of cultural interest in Britain, the skill to match tourist facilities to the needs of fictional families, checking suitability for disabled people, selecting and rearranging information, searching web-sites, writing letters and evaluating their own work.

Another unusual feature of the curriculum is the GCSE Law course. This relates partly to career aspirations but is also deeply grounded in the concerns of the community for protecting legal rights on matters concerning housing and immigration. The learning is based on problem-solving activities, and the onus is firmly placed on the students. The teacher rarely writes on the board himself, as students are asked to demonstrate. The difficulties in obtaining legal rights are clearly drawn out – that defamation can only be judged in the High Court, a rich people's court with no legal aid. Students are asked how this could be overcome. 'Abolish the jury? But why do juries exist?' The students learn to make sharp and subtle logical distinctions and develop ethical and social understanding. There is a great deal of positive feedback and an ethos of courtesy : 'Next week we're going to study...Thank you for coming'. A remarkable 75 per cent of candidates gained A*-C grades last year.

Curriculum as social and cultural development

The headteacher pointed to the tension between an instrumental view of education, which she saw as the major tendency in the National Curriculum, and a genuinely educational and developmental perspective.

> We have to give them the kind of experience which is sharp about certificates, because they admit them to higher things and make them feel good, but we've tried not to lose other valuable things. We used to run a one-hour session for activities during Key Stage 3, a sort of

youth club in school hours, for which teachers had to nominate personal interests which were not linked to their main specialism. So we could offer yoga or environment, or a dance club for Year 7 boys. This year we've switched to a Focus Day every half-term, with activities for particular year groups. For younger students, these are often adventurous activities, such as the Murder Mystery, which culminates in the local police coming in to arrest a teacher. That goes down well! For older students, it could be a Leadership Day, with various problem-solving activities, or the Health Conference. These are often supported from outside, but relate to our philosophy of *Learning Together.*

Current examples of focus days include rock-climbing and other outdoor activities, combined arts days, creating a banquet, and field-work for various subjects. The Year 10 Health Day brings in quality professionals and displays; the Peugeot Industry Day is an industrial simulation; the Leadership Challenge covers planning for improvements in school premises, a survival exercise, pitching tents in the wind, and involves reflection about group dynamics. For senior students, the days also include careers and mock interviews.

The Murder Mystery is a good example of a focus day supported by Birmingham's 'University of the First Age' – one of their *Super Learning Days*. Students are encouraged to reflect on the quality of their learning – 'Learning is fun, and I'm a superlearner' – and a multi-sensory approach based on Howard Gardner's theory of multiple intelligences.

In another day based on *Macbeth*, students rotated round a circus of workshops – visual, kinaesthetic, intrapersonal, interpersonal. Fifty students then chose to be part of a six-week project, then there was another day to look at the production side, including publicity and staging. One student even phoned Buckingham Palace to invite the queen! Finally, over a long weekend, there was an extended rehearsal, a sleepover in the library, and the play was performed on the Monday.

The Senior Teacher (Curriculum) expressed his concern, shared with the University of the First Age team, lest these special events become a 'black hole for innovative energy, for teachers frustrated by the National Curriculum' (Tim Boyes). They had to feed into the mainstream curriculum. There has been INSET on the theory of multiple intelligences but it is 'easier to accept these ideas as psychological theory than to put them into practice'.

The University of the First Age also organises summer schools on a university campus, including those supporting primary-secondary transition, and short courses (e.g. two hours a week for 4 or 6 weeks) on subjects that are not part of the school curriculum, such as astronomy or salsa. In addition, they were instrumental in launching 'Playing for Success' (study centres based on football clubs).

There is a special quality to inter-school cooperation in Birmingham. The head of science spoke of pulling in agencies to develop greater opportunities:

> Teachers from various schools worked with British Waterways, putting on an event which involved 1200 children over a fortnight. There were activities involving building an arch bridge, the bonding of walls, surveying, an architectural walk. Our students designed a solar-powered narrow-boat.
>
> We work with primary schools who haven't got specialist equipment, and this leads to staff development and greater understanding. We're now planning for a Year of Science and Technology. The advisers launched the idea by asking teachers how they wanted to do it. Teachers with particular interests formed working groups. In departments, we make sure all teachers understand that their ideas are valued.
>
> It's really important to provide a rich curriculum for students in this area and we need the money to get students out. I'm concerned, nationally, that competition between schools has damaged collegiality between teachers and that performance pay will destroy team effort within schools too. (John Legg)

Later that day, I met a young Asian woman science teacher, who'd been at a meeting with female engineers at Jaguar to encourage more girls into engineering. Taster courses and workshadowing were planned.

The head of Creative Arts spoke of the importance of arts in raising achievement. 'As in technology, students see concrete outcomes. Their success is demonstrable. There are alternative forms of expression to writing, and it develops the mind for other things'. The outcomes are indeed present throughout the city, as a result of projects with artists and museums. GCSE Art results are excellent, with three quarters achieving A*-C grades. There are two drama option groups each year, and music is being redeveloped. Visual arts are a sensitive area for some Muslims but parents take pride in seeing their children's work displayed and are increasingly understanding the career potentials. Perhaps because of some anxieties about human images, there appeared to be a marked variety of media (pottery, textiles, batik, etc.) and a richness of other types of representation, such as human hands, still life, plants, design and buildings.

An English lesson I saw shortly before the Key Stage 3 tests illustrated a number of curricular values: ingenuity in finding curricular solutions despite National Curriculum pressures; the search for deep learning rather than superficial 'cramming'; an engagement with popular culture; and a multisensory approach. The teacher was concerned that students' responses to written texts didn't seem to distinguish *how* from *what*. The class looked at last year's test, an extract from H.G.Wells' *War of the Worlds* in which the narrator is awaiting the creature's emergence from the spaceship. They looked at the way the narrator's reactions changed, the writer's choice of physical details, the description of the Martian's behaviour, and the use of comparisons. Then the lesson switched to film, for a close study of the opening of *Startrek Insurrection*.

'First let's answer the what. What do you see in the village?' The students identify the images of a blissful rural community – children playing, farming, baking bread. 'Now let's look at the decisions the director has made.' They explore the unusual overlap between the theme tune and the Paramount sign, the dramatic shift in the music, the use of camera angles to create expectations and to signal a contrast between good and evil, innocence and villainy. They talk about the music in other films, in 'Jaws', in horror films. 'If you switch the music off, you just see the woman going upstairs. Because of the music, we know it's dangerous, but she doesn't.'

The head of English pointed to the cultural role of English and Media Studies.

There's a meeting of cultures. Students' home and heritage cultures are reinforced, and there's also a broadening through other cultures. Both are important... Students have a right to texts from cultures they understand – cultures in the plural, because they might know more about David Beckham than Mohammed...The agencies policing English don't seem to understand issues of culture. Our students sitting last year's test found the passage about the Loch Ness Monster completely inaccessible! Our students like Shakespeare, because they can engage with the issues, but the tests are encouraging an unbalanced concentration on a few scenes...The current focus on 'literacy' is too narrow. A lot of English is about exploring identity and this is closely bound up with developing critical reading, which is a crucial aspect of literacy. It doesn't go unnoticed by our students, of course, that the idyllic villagers in the Startrek episode are all white. (Peter Weir)

Meeting all needs

A flexible attitude is taken towards setting, with variations between subjects. Maths and science are set and there is some setting in technology, but other subjects such as the arts, PE and IT are mixed ability. English and humanities group into two broad bands.

The school has taken part in the pilot of the National Literacy Programme for secondary schools and there have been measurable gains in progress. There has been a weekly reading lesson but literacy is being embedded into subjects, with schemes of work showing the type of text for which each subject is responsible. The education authority's four consultants have worked intensively with departments to achieve this.

There is always a worry when bilingual students are subsumed under 'Special Needs' or 'Learning Support'. Here, a combined 'Language and Learning Support Department' has the clarity and expertise to diagnose specific needs. They feel able to tell after about six weeks whether a new bilingual student has special educational needs, and are critical of unnecessary delays in securing statements. Their work has shifted heavily towards literacy and they collaborate in the University of the First Age summer schools, the Key Stage 3 reading programme, provision of book boxes, literacy screening of new students, and staff development, especially with English and humanities teachers.

Some students have an agreed withdrawal from normal curriculum for two hours a week for a whole year, while maintaining curricular access through a focus on subject-related texts rather than generic remedial texts. Staffing is intensive – three teachers to twenty students; there is a sharp focus on the textual features, layout and syntax of different subject texts; and very rapid improvement – students often making 6-9 months' progress in two months.

In a Science lesson I saw a careful revision of the key activities of animals (respiration, excretion etc.) in which learning the right word was carefully grounded in understanding of the concept. There were frequent references to everyday experiences – jumping back when you touch a saucepan, little brothers getting bigger. The teacher emphasised that the technical vocabulary is important not only for passing exams but also for understanding when you read a newspaper or watch the television. 'If you don't know the word, you won't know what's going on.'

Golden Hillock is involved in the national *Gifted and Talented* initiative and believes that Birmingham's work on curriculum enhancement, preferred learning styles and multiple intelligences offers a way of avoiding the danger of elitism. The school is required to nominate particular students but other students are also involved in activities as appropriate. Selection is based not only on non-verbal reasoning scores but also on staff nominating students with particular talents. The school is planning to question students about their interests and hobbies during the induction process. The opportunities provided are varied and often not traditionally 'academic' – for instance, a filming course involving planning, writing, performing, filming and editing. The coordinator is keen to use the initiative to develop mainstream lessons as well as special provision, so that there is greater opportunity for independent learning and an end to the practice of giving more able students extra work to complete after they finish the main task.

Conclusion

One of the most impressive features of Golden Hillock school, along with the ethos for learning and the quality of relationships, is the thoughtfulness with which staff have addressed development issues, from site management to curriculum. Everyone I spoke to, including the student representatives, impressed me with their reflectiveness and their ability to link a specific issue or the teaching of a particular lesson to wider social perspectives and deep-seated principles. Social reflectiveness combines philosophy with commitment and the search for a better future. The school's motto 'Learning Together' also sums up the school's development process.

With particular thanks to Thelma Probert (Headteacher), Don Smith and Eileen Brown (Deputy Heads), Wendy Sharples (Vocational Activities), Jerry Whitehouse (Law), Tim Boyes (Senior Teacher Curriculum), John Legg (Science), Keith Tomlinson (Creative Arts), Sam Padbury and Peter Weir (English) and Creina Holland (Science).

Sparrow Hill Community School, Rochdale

Sparrow Hill is a large primary school in central Rochdale, on the edge of Greater Manchester. Over 90 per cent of the pupils come from the Asian community of Pakistani origin, which settled in the town centre area in the 1950s and 60s. Many families are devout Muslims. The school includes a small number of white pupils who live in the central area, some of whose parents have been attracted by the ethos and reputation of the school and have made a deliberate decision for their children to attend this multiethnic school. Rochdale is quite sharply divided between the central areas of nineteenth century terraced houses, where most Asian families have settled, and the surrounding white suburbs.

Education is highly valued in this community. This is partly related to the moral seriousness of Muslim culture, with its traditional respect for learning. It is also a consequence of the history of the community after settling in Rochdale. The original settlers came with high expectations of work in the textile industry but this soon entered a period of sharp decline and disappointments set in which have had a lasting impact on morale. The community works closely with the school, which they know respects their culture and strives to better their children's opportunities.

Sparrow Hill School is split between two sites, about a quarter of a mile apart. The education authority provided a new building, which houses the nursery and early years, but it is the older building, housing Years 3-6 and the community centre, that is situated at the heart of the community. Headteacher David How is keen to develop the school at this latter site, in order to strengthen the community links.

The school is quite large, with two classes per year, although numbers have declined from their earlier peak of nearly 70 per year.

There is a nursery class, taking different pupils in the afternoon from the morning. The community centre is busy and has always been popular among the women, many of them mothers of children at the school. Most of the staff are very attached to the school, and the majority have taught there for between 10 and 20 years. Many of the staff, especially teaching assistants and clerical staff, are Asian women who have grown up in the area.

According to the official quantitative data, Sparrow Hill is a rapidly improving school. The DfEE's 'measure of improvement' (a total of the number of pupils achieving level 4 or above in each of the core subjects at age 11, divided by the number of eligible pupils) shows a rise from 76 in 1996 to 131 in 1999. The change nationally was much smaller, from 170 to 215. In 1999, 54 per cent achieved level 4 in English. This is around the average for the 'benchmark group' (i.e. given the free meals ratio), and shows impressive progress given the limited English of the children at the age of five. But the school's achievements cannot simply be measured in terms of official statistics, as I hope to show. The pupils' creativity, learning skills and social development are important aspects of the school's achievement.

A community within a community

The community centre is located on the lower floor of the older building, underneath the junior classrooms. For many years, it has provided a social centre for Asian women. (The men have tended to gather at the mosque and in another community centre nearby.) In the 1980s, for example, it was mainly used for leisure activities and classes, such as sewing and keep-fit. It has also served as a source of advice at various times and is used for community-run events such as the Meena Bazaar (a clothes sale and fashion parade) and Qawali concerts.

In the past ten years, however, the local women have been making different demands, and they have been supported in this by the professional community workers paid by the town council as well as their own representatives on the community council. The social events are still important, but the majority of courses nowadays lead to qualifications. As the head pointed out, the school has responded to the changing needs of the local community. There are currently nearly 50 courses, and the present list is very broad, including:

- A-level Urdu and Arabic, ESOL, and Interpreters' Certificates

- Access courses in Sociology and Psychology, leading to university entrance

- Business English

- Word-processing and other IT courses

- Classroom Assistants' Certificate, Family Literacy, and NVQ Childcare

- Multicultural Fashion and Design

- Cookery

- Teacher Training

- Keep Fit for Women

- Music

- First Aid at Work

Many of the courses are run by the local FE college but are held at the community school, since the women find it more comfortable and convenient to pursue their education here. Many courses are free and the concessionary rates for the higher qualification courses are modest, at around £5 per term. Every effort has been made to commission courses to meet a demand, and most courses take place during the school day.

One characteristic of the local community has been the determination of girls and young women to overcome barriers to education and career development. It is a well established pattern in the local secondary schools that the Asian girls are the highest achieving group, and young women make an important contribution to the family income through outside employment. Young mothers and older women have now taken a lead from them and are keen to pursue new opportunities, sometimes in spite of opposition from more traditional male relatives. Older gender-based inequalities and assumptions are gradually being overcome.

This in turn has helped to raise achievement in the school. The children know that lifelong learning is a real issue in their families, and they have a role model in their own mothers and aunts. They know that qualifications are in reach and that education is vital to their future opportunities.

There is a direct link between some of the courses and the life of the school. The school, mainly in its nursery and Key Stage 1 classes, provides short-term placements for participants in the courses for classroom assistants, and often more permanent employment after that. Mothers attending the family literacy course play an increasing part in reading in the classroom, as well as at home. These experiences give families a greater understanding of the life of the school and help to bridge the gap between teaching and learning styles in the school and the more traditional patterns experienced by mothers educated in Pakistan or the style of the classes at the local mosques.

It may be difficult for people who have little knowledge of the Asian communities of northern England to appreciate the importance of this bridge-building. Partly as a result of high levels of unemployment here, the Muslim communities of Lancashire and West Yorkshire have tended to be inward-looking, and sometimes feel uncertain about whether it was wise to settle in Britain. The communities remain close-knit, their lives focused around the mosques and Asian supermarkets, and many young children have little contact with non-Asians. In this context, the school's community status has been extremely important in the struggle to raise achievement, and has led, for example, to more children experiencing the pleasure of reading at home before they come to school.

An appreciation of the strength of the Muslim heritage is a major feature of teachers' professionalism. I visited the school early in Ramadan. It was understood and acknowledged that many of the older children were fasting. Sandwiches to take home were provided for children on free meals. Two quiet rooms had been designated, one for boys and one for girls, but the constant rain meant that all the children had to stay indoors. Nevertheless, the atmosphere in all the classrooms was peaceful, and children were contented playing with board games, reading books and generally chatting. Children were told that, provided they had a note from their parents, they would be able to attend Friday afternoon prayers at the mosque, where some of the boys had been chosen as readers.

The Muslim culture has an influence on many of the school's activities but the school is careful to reflect the fact that its children are growing up with a share of other British cultures too. The teachers know the value of cultural diversity and understand that their lives may seem to span two worlds. A large mural produced for Ramadan and Eid dominates the school hall, beautifully designed by the older pupils in the form of mosques made out of shiny coloured foil; by its side stands a brightly decorated fir tree. Close by, children are working at computers.

It is the school's skill at negotiating the two cultures which is so important in developing confident and dynamic youngsters who are enthusiastic about learning. The pupils realise that most of their teachers are non-Muslim and that Islam is not the dominant faith in Britain but they grow in the security that it is respected and supported in their school.

The culture of respect also pervades the relationships among pupils and between pupils and staff. At the end of the literacy hour, I saw a class of nine-year-olds sitting on the carpet for a 'calming down time', where they were invited to nominate others who'd been kind to them and reflect on whether they'd been able to kind to other people. Boys as well as girls engaged thoughtfully in this process, showing no hint of 'macho' toughness. The parallel class were politely invited to enter their cards in a competition. When some pupils failed to listen quietly during a science lesson, the teacher's appeal was based on rationality and the need to learn, not on power: 'I'm finding this really difficult. If you talk, I can't concentrate. I forget what I'm saying, and then the lesson gets boring for everybody.'

There was a remarkably calm atmosphere in the school, even though the weather had prevented the children from playing outside for nearly a fortnight. The teacher stopped herself from organising turns to choose a game: 'I'm not going to say 'It's your turn', but you should just go when you're ready. Get your work tidied away first, then go and choose a game, because I know there's not going to be a rush, you're much too sensible.'

Valuing achievement

Many schools have schemes for rewarding achievement, such as merit tokens and praise at assemblies, and Sparrow Hill is no exception, but the notable feature here is the way in which the learning itself is a source of pride. This is how schools genuinely create an ethos of achievement.

The teachers of the two Year 4 classes have been able to turn the structures of the numeracy and literacy hours to advantage. Building on existing patterns of classroom organisation in the school, they have provided a public arena for sharing individual thinking.

The numeracy hour in one class opened with a game in which a dice was thrown to generate six digits, which the children then had to order to make the largest or the smallest possible number. Each child was engaged in thinking at great speed, creating a collective buzz of excitement. Then someone (not always the fastest) was asked to the front to write the number on the board and to speak it aloud. The higher achievers did so confidently, and the teacher scaffolded the process for others by gradually uncovering the tens, then hundreds, and so on, so that the child could build up the number.

There were other interesting features of the cognitive development being developed during the numeracy hour. The game preceded the instructional session, raising the level of mental alertness. Without having all six digits, pupils were asked to predict where might be the best place for a 2 or a 6. The calendar used for the second part of the lesson was clearly related to real life – a tool for marking the dates of Eid, of visits to the dentist and so on. The abler pupils at maths were given different individual tasks, involving working out number patterns on the calendar. There was a rapid interchange of activities during the 45 minutes devoted to maths, ending with another game: eyes closed, putting up your hand when you think 45 seconds had elapsed – another real-life application of numeracy. Throughout all this time, the bilingual classroom assistant was actively supporting children's learning, working flexibly with groups and individuals as required, and often assuming a whole-class role.

I was able to observe a Year 4 science lesson about the solar system. Here too, there was a judicious use of different grouping patterns: whole-class, groups and individual learning. The school, like many progressive primary schools, had always devoted a good deal of time to individual research, but now the pace was faster and it took place within a more public frame. The session began with an interactive exposition on the orbits of the planets and their moons and ended with pupils presenting and explaining to the class the notes they had taken. The demonstration at the start provided a clear cognitive framework for exploring some of the details. It was reinforced by the teacher working closely with a group which she suspected had not fully understood. Pupils clearly gained in self-esteem and confidence from presenting their key facts to the rest of the class. The teacher's verbal presentation to this class of mainly EAL pupils was strongly supported by visual props – lively facial expressions, diagrams, pictures. Care was taken to ensure that each group had the texts they needed in order to explore the details of the sun or the moon or Jupiter. There was a clear focus on language development, with these nine-year-olds confidently and intelligently using words such as atmosphere and hemisphere.

The literacy hour

Some of the 'model' versions of the literacy hour shown during official training sessions were criticised by teachers at the school for focusing overmuch on technicalities of grammar. Some lessons presented on video as good models were considered to be deeply flawed because of the way the 'naming of the parts' diverted pupils from active engagement with the text in the search for meaning. Also, the teachers feared that reading was being disconnected from writing and spoken language and that these latter could be neglected.

The Year 4 teachers were enthusiastic about the literacy hour but regarded it as something they had to adapt for their children. Technical terms (adverbs, infer, flashback and so on) were being used, but specifically as an aid to reading actively and enabling more powerful writing and speaking. There was a strong semantic focus as well as the syntactic one. Many bilingual pupils, even at age 16, are confident with the everyday or literal meanings of words but weaker in their command of more figurative uses of language. Language is seen as denotative but not connotative. Both Year 4 teachers were using the literacy hour to focus on building up a rich and resonant vocabulary for their pupils.

The whole-class commencement to the morning's literacy hour had in a sense begun with story-telling at the end of the previous afternoon. This had all the pleasure of the best primary school story-telling but was made active by the teacher's invitations to predict. The reading of a short mystery story called 'Tremors' was truly dramatic. Inviting the pupils to take an active role added to the mood of suspense, rather than being a distraction. 'What do you think is going to happen now?...What's the writer just dropped in? What are you thinking?...What made you say that? Anybody else?' These were invitations to contribute and engage, rather than teacherly questions requiring paraphrase or recall. Direct questions were actually relatively rare in this session; much more frequent were the teacher's authentic reactions to the text, exclamations rather than questions, which invited, modelled and developed pupils' own responses. 'Oh now you've got me even more worried!' 'Oh so you think....?!' The teacher explained afterwards that she tried to make reading to the class like a parent reading to a young child at home – evoking shared responses, actively bringing the text to life, relating personally to the story, and never a test.

On the Friday morning, the literacy hour (or English, as the pupils rightly call it) was an exploration of how to begin a story, a development of vocabulary and a preparation for writing. It included whole class and small group work but didn't follow a rigid pattern. The children were looking together at the cover of a 'big book', *Ghost Dog*. They discussed the purpose of the opening to such a story, suggesting ideas such as the need to 'hook the reader' and to establish the genre. They focused on different images on the cover illustration, the teacher writing on the board pupils' suggestions for descriptive words and phrases, with those deriving from inference rather than observation written in blue: *dog with red eye...glowing red eye... red laser eyes.... mad threatening laser eyes... ghost dog...*

One pupil suggests beaming. The teacher gently steers her from this, explaining that beaming has happy connotations, the beaming sun.

The trees are '*spiky... leafless... stretching... shivering...*' Teacher: 'Good, you've started to infer. You can't tell directly if it's cold or windy, but it's a scary night, so you decided it's cold. Let's put it in blue.' Soon pupils are insisting on blue for ideas they have inferred rather than seen. At first, the teacher rejects the adjective *blaring* for the moon but then she warms to it, explaining its associations with loud music and agreeing that this will enrich the description : the '*blaring yellow moon*' is an improvement on '*the big yellow bold moon*'.

The process is open and supportive. The more imaginative and articulate pupils are able to make good progress and model the process for others with a narrower command of English. With the help of this scaffolding, all the pupils take part in an exploration of descriptive language, with frequent similes and metaphors. Pupils then continue this in groups, this time using illustrations from Michael Moorcroft's science fiction stories, and eventually each group has the opportunity to share their ideas with the class. The group work is an intensive search for the right expression. To ring the changes during the sharing of ideas, the other groups have to guess which picture is being described.

The display on *Macbeth* confirms the value of this approach to English. Nominally, this is the literacy hour, and it would be pedantic to conclude that it didn't meet the quasi-statutory requirements. But this is much richer, closely linked to the best traditions of English teaching in primary and secondary schools. The study of *Macbeth*, an ambitious choice, has been supported by workshops run by visiting members of the Royal Shakespeare Company. The pupils' poems are testimony to the value of the balance of support and freedom they receive – not a contradiction between structure and creativity but structures used to foster creativity. Every poem based on an acrostic of Lady Macbeth was quite different but the children have drawn on a shared experience, part of which involves digging into a rich source of vocabulary, somewhat archaic but heroic and resonant. One example:

> Lady Macbeth was excited when she read the letter.
> A really crazy thought came into her mind.
> Desperate to talk to her husband about her black desires,
> Yearning to be king and queen.

Macbeth was not sure what to do.
Anxiously say no, and not love her, or say yes.
Coward, she cried.
Be the innocent flower on the outside,
but be the serpent under it...

Or these two poems about the witches:

Hideous screams from the battlefield
echo dreadfully across the heath.
Torrents of rain rushed down from the filthy grey clouds.
Thunder deadened the screams.
A huge ball of smoke rose up
Revealing three skeletal bodies
dancing round and round.
He heard a witch say his name,
Then one shrieked,
Macbeth!

* * *

Swirling smoke still drifted
from the distant battlefield,
As lightning thrashed the heath.
A thick mist cleared,
Revealing the shape of three bony witches.
Wild glittering eyes glowed red
from their faces, shrivelled like rotten fruit.
Their weird voices cackled loudly
Waking up the darkness.

The parallel class had been reading Berlie Doherty's *Children of Winter*, a novel which takes the characters and the reader back into the time of the plague. The plenary part of the literacy hour had, in effect, begun the previous day, when the pupils watched a video in which professional poets demonstrated some simple techniques, including a 'found poem'. In pairs, the children discussed ideas and phrases from the novel on which they would like to focus.

On the Friday morning, each pair quickly settled to reread a chosen chapter, highlighting sentences and phrases which they thought were particularly meaningful. This involved an active style of reading, selective and focused. The pupils then used these to develop a *found poem* within a simple structure, based on a chorus and echo effect. As always, the teacher and bilingual assistant were circulating round the groups, providing just enough support for the process but without undermining the children's independence. One of the groups chose as a chorus the quotation '*Over the stile and into the past*' (a play with words – past, not path). One of the children reminded the class of the term 'flashback' – another example of technical terms used to heighten reading, rather than texts being used as the excuse to teach technical terms. The following poem was generated quite quickly, in about 40 minutes including rereading the original chapter, with no opportunity to redraft. It isn't as mature a piece of writing as the examples based on *Macbeth*, but has its own resonance and sensitivity and is an empathetic and creative response to the novel. It should be read aloud to bring out the different voices implicit in the text.

Over the stile and into the past.
Over the stile and into the past.
No, there's lots of Tebbutts around here,
                Tebbutts around here.

It's a local name
      local name.

Over the stile and into the past.
Over the stile and into the past.
There's an old barn
      old barn.
We could shelter in there
      shelter in there.
Over the stile and into the past.
Over the stile and into the past.
It's an old cruck-barn
      old cruck-barn.
Look at those cobwebs.
      those cobwebs.
Over the stile and into the past.
Over the stile and into the past.

They look as if they've been here a few centuries.
              been here a few centuries.

Over the stile and into the past.
Over the stile and into the past.
Why did the old place give such a strange feeling of security
                                    such a strange feeling of security
And such a terrible feeling of loss.
                        feeling of loss.

Towards the end, various pairs of children read aloud their poems. One hesitant reader had only got as far as the collecting stage but gained visibly in confidence and self-esteem by reading her phrases aloud to the class with the support assistant. Here was a climate in which children supported each other to overcome difficulties, and she received ample praise and applause from her classmates.

A discussion took place about various ways of improving the poems and how they were read. The children then entered a thoughtful discussion about the sentence, 'Other children had gone before she had time to mourn'.

Discussions about the literacy hour

A major reason for the success of these sessions is the culture of reflection among Sparrow Hill teachers. Sparrow Hill has long enjoyed a reputation in the LEA for curriculum development, as well as for its positive ethos and closeness to the community it serves. It was clear from my conversations with various teachers that its continued development was closely linked to a culture of reflectiveness.

> Our curriculum for language development used to be based on experience, but now it's based on texts. Before, we had control over contexts but not over skills. Now we expose pupils systematically to strategies, whether it's reading or calculations. We aim much more consciously for cognitive development. There's a danger, though, of losing the direct experience. (Rupert Twogood)

Because of these long-established habits of evaluating and theorising, the school is able to take the best features from national initiatives while avoiding the pitfalls.

> The art is to see how one kind of activity can be made to work for another, i.e. speaking, reading and writing complement one another, but many teachers in other schools will be doing each in isolation. There's even been a book marketed called *101 Literacy Hours*, and

> teachers are just walking into class and delivering an off-the-peg literacy hour, completely out of context. (Bev MacGowan)

Curriculum innovation on a national level only works to the extent to which it is negotiated at a local level and integrated into a healthy school culture.

> It's been successful here because of the processes of staff development and school development we've been through. The head opened up the agenda, asking staff to say what they really valued. We were already working on the First Steps programme, which was the inspiration behind the Literacy Strategy, and so we understood the new methods in depth. (Bev MacGowan)

Teachers were generally enthusiastic about the literacy strategy but avoided dogmatism in the manner of its implementation. Thus, there was flexibility in the timing and sequencing of sessions, the belief that the texts must be of good quality and meaningful to the children, and an interweaving of literacy with other areas of the curriculum such as Science and History.

The school has readily seized upon the positive features of the strategy. It has:

> brought more rigour, made us more systematic. It's given new opportunities for developing self-esteem, through the public nature of the event, and has helped raise expectations, enabling pupils to talk about language, using words such as *flashback*... It's given teachers and pupils a better understanding of linguistic structures and genre. (David How)

Many primary teachers have had access for the first time to these linguistic and literary concepts, and here they were certainly using them to advantage. Yet there were features of the way in which the literacy hour has been imposed nationally that were disquieting. Teachers of the younger children were particularly anxious that there was now less time for spoken language and for developing a broader understanding of the world. They had noticed that the younger children were often tired by the afternoon and tended towards less creative low-level activities with sand and water. Structured play, once a strength of the infants department at Sparrow Hill, still existed and was linked to literacy and numeracy but it was much weaker than before. There was some relief that the revised early years curriculum, at national level, had reaffirmed the importance of play.

The school has benefited from well-established structures of staff development, both internally and through the LEA's Section 11 service *LEAP.* The EAL teachers, although well established on the school staff, belonged to the LEAP service and they were released for many Wednesday afternoons during the year for in-service and resource development work at the centre. This was seen as enriching their contribution to the school's development. Some teachers felt that the *cascaded* official training for the literacy hour had often been of a different kind – tightly scheduled, dictated from above, while questions such as '*what about our EAL children?*' were overruled and ignored and no time for discussion was allowed.

Before the National Curriculum, the school's curriculum was developed with close attention to multicultural and antiracist issues. This was still the school's philosophy, but the speed with which teachers had been confronted with new agendas meant that opportunities were being missed. The revised National Curriculum would restore opportunities, within recognised units, to choose topics which linked to the experiences of the children; however, some teachers felt that the new non-statutory schemes of work for History and Geography had been adopted by the staff 'on the nod' because the teachers were so tired, and they had accepted topics such as the history of seaside holidays, which were remote from the Asian community's experience.

The power to learn
It is hard to sum up the reasons for a school like Sparrow Hill's success. It certainly cannot be reduced to a formula. Some qualities, however, stand out.

- The pupils here are full of enthusiasm for learning. They are open to new experiences and new challenges, and move forward in the confidence that they can achieve.

- The teachers are brimful of ideas and ambition for these children. Their relationships, classroom organisation and teaching methods build self-esteem, develop confidence as learners and raise expectations. The discourse of their relationship with the children and of the teaching and learning is often closer to that of the children's lives than of traditional schooling.

- The staff collectively – teachers, bilingual assistants, community workers, EAL specialists, secretaries and the rest – have a close understanding of and warm empathy with the life of the Asian community. They appreciate its ambitions for education, its cultural roots and its caring ethos. They also understand the economic and social disappointments which the community has faced since settling in Northern England, as traditional industries have collapsed and not been replaced. A school cannot avoid or overcome these problems but it can develop confident, articulate, co-operative and socially-aware young people who have the tools to learn throughout their lives.

Sparrow Hill School is an achieving school, in the broadest sense. Achievement is collectively valued at every level. Children support each other in overcoming obstacles to learning. On the second day of my visit, great pleasure was taken by the teacher and pupils when a ten-year-old boy who tended only to whisper in school found the confidence to read aloud to the whole class. Inclusiveness is a culture built by pupils, parents and teachers working together. High achievement is a source of collective pride and genuine celebration, be it poems on *Macbeth* or boys being chosen to read in the mosque.

Developing a school which empowers children in these ways requires a special quality of management – their teachers, other staff and the parents must also feel empowered. Control mechanisms such as lesson monitoring and evaluating test results play a part but their role is only meaningful and effective within a collective vision, a culture of professional reflection, the building of the school community within the wider community, a vision of what these children can achieve.

Above all, the power to learn cannot be fostered in a school culture which divorces two learning cultures. Sparrow Hill's success in teaching the skills and knowledge needed for growing up in the modern world depends upon the school valuing the living heritage of the local Pakistani community, itself in flux. The EAL service's principles set the tone:

- supporting the development of bilingualism, recognising its positive advantages and fostering the use of mother tongue

- building on pupils' previous knowledge, skills and experience, and creating a learning environment which positively fosters them.

Sparrow Hill's pupils are learning how to move fluently between two languages, two cultures, many cultures, many worlds, and into a different future.

With particular thanks to David How (Headteacher), Kathy Allan and Bev MacGowan (Year 4 and Literacy).

PART C – THE CONCLUSION
... and some ways forward

My first instinct in planning this book was to dispense with a conclusion altogether. I wanted the stories of the ten schools to speak for themselves and inspire others. I have been particularly keen to avoid producing a bullet-point list of 'Key Characteristics of Effective Schools'. Lists of this kind easily become counterproductive if they short-circuit thoughtful debate about the purpose of education and pre-empt the discussions in the whole school community which build a shared vision and sense of purpose.

Nevertheless, the common threads which have emerged in these stories of successful schools are too important to allow them to fray. Together they lead towards an understanding of educational processes and school development which will hopefully empower schools elsewhere, and give other young people the power to learn.

Leadership and school development
In researching and writing this book, I was determined to avoid the excessive focus on the headteacher role, which has characterised most writing on school effectiveness and improvement. My evidence on school development processes has been drawn from a wider range of sources, including interviews with a substantial number of teachers and other staff, frequently enriched by incidental glimpses of school development processes gained when looking at something else.

This is not to imply that the headteacher is unimportant. In all these schools, the head has played a determining role in making the school what it is today. It is simply that many other individuals have also played important leadership roles, and the success must be attributed to all the players. Time and again, when I probed the reasons for the school's success, the head would say 'the staff', and the staff would say 'the pupils'.

All ten headteachers proved to be memorable individuals, with rare qualities of empathy and professional imagination. Each has developed a close feeling for the communities their schools serve. One particularly helpful metaphor for their styles of leadership is Steve White's notion of the *helicopter mind*. They are able to alternate between rising high enough to scan the horizon, to see the location of their school in time and place so as to develop a vision; and involving themselves deeply and intensively in specific events and change processes.

Given the extent of involvement many of them have in the local community, engaging in activities well beyond any possible job description, it is remarkable that each has such a direct presence in their school, among the staff and pupils. They are well known and available to their colleagues and pupils, and for some pupils they virtually *symbolise* the school.

Effective headteachers and senior management teams need to have clear management *information*. They need to be able to evaluate all the processes which affect the well-being and success of pupils. They particularly need to keep a sharp eye on achievement and on the quality of teaching and learning. Essential tools for this are an analysis of assessment data, the direct observation of lessons, and annual review meetings with middle managers and departments. However, efficient use of these tools is not in itself enough, and can even be counterproductive. These key management processes are only effective when grounded in a positive staff culture – a shared ambition to provide the best possible education for the pupils. And successful headteachers are influential in building such a staff culture.

The monitoring processes must be conducted sensitively and without arrogance or they will backfire. School managers need to be trusted and, while they should have high expectations of the staff and be prepared to challenge low achievement and complacency, they must show high regard for their colleagues. Successful headteachers also understand that their colleagues have their individual professional and personal histories; that they are subject to stress and strain as well as elation and excitement and at times need sensitive support; and that a development plan which overloads individuals will inevitably collapse like a pack of cards.

The successful school leader is a good listener and a good learner, with an intelligent understanding of curriculum, teaching and learning, relationships and pastoral processes, and the imagination and creativity to find new solutions which will fit the current needs of the school.

I am deliberately not writing separate comments on the qualities of deputy heads and other members of senior management teams because what I have said about headteachers applies to them too. In each of the schools visited, even within the constraints of a two or three day visit, it became clear that other key individuals – deputy heads, specific subject leaders, team leaders, EAL coordinators, individual teachers, home-school liaison workers and so on – had crucial leadership roles and particular strengths which often complemented those of the headteacher. It is vital to effective school development that the relationships and structures encourage the emergence and practice of leadership and creativity in different quarters.

I did not have the time or opportunity to explore the role of other agencies in the development of these ten schools but it is apparent that some very effective relationships had been built with education authorities and in some cases universities. The political reform of the 1988 Act almost wiped out *inter-school co-operation*, and it was a particular delight to see that this is still very much in evidence, in Birmingham in particular. The parallel initiatives of the Children's University and the University of the First Age are extremely exciting and are clearly having an impact on broadening the educational experience and raising achievement.

The political mindset which has overemphasised the vertical dimension of school improvement processes has neglected horizontal relationships of *partnership and teamwork*. A monitoring visit to observe and evaluate a teacher at work may occur once a year but horizontal collaboration happens every day. As well as the whole staff, smaller teams develop in many different forms in schools – around subjects, age groups, pastoral roles, development issues. The school's success grows through the collective reflection, morale-building, personal sustenance, resource writing, lesson planning and vision-building of small and large teams.

Teachers who have to plan education around issues of language, race and poverty need this quality of co-operation to survive and thrive. They have to develop novel solutions, write original resources, plan and trial lessons which engage and motivate pupils who could easily become demoralised. Top-down command structures are no substitute for *commitment, enthusiasm and shared vision*. You cannot compel optimism or order teachers to have faith in the future.

The role of language development teachers is particularly crucial, and I came across evidence of strong teamwork between EAL specialists and mainstream teachers. Establishing these partnerships requires sensitivity, and regular meetings take time, but their abundant fruits include:

• more effective resourcing and lesson planning

• greater daring in trying out new ideas

• the inclusion of previously marginalised pupils in classroom processes

• enhanced reflection on learning and fine-tuning of teaching methods

• a closer attention to individual strengths and needs

• and a focused attention on linguistic and cognitive processes.

Successful teamwork depends upon and engenders reflection about deeper principles and values. It is a key aspect of informal staff development. More formal staff development shares many of the same characteristics. It has to be an occasion for *reflection about values and theories, for evaluating practice as well as learning from theory, for sharing good practice within and beyond the school, for generating new ideas, and for planning their implementation.* Joyce and Showers (1988) appropriate the term 'coaching' for the close guidance within the classroom that effective implementation often requires, especially when it involves a significant shift of teaching style. This has taken many forms, including some of the best practice of LEA advisory teachers in the early 1990s or, more recently, of literacy and numeracy consultants. In general, coaching is not strongly developed in our education systems but variants of it are visible in schools, particularly involving language development teachers in partnership with mainstream staff.

The curriculum and extra-curricular activities

The school improvement literature of the 1990s repeatedly talks about teachers '*delivering* the curriculum'. In England and Wales, the National Curriculum (with its capital letters) was imposed by Margaret Thatcher's education minister Kenneth Baker as a rigid definition of the content, concepts and activities to be covered in each Key Stage. It was technologically forward-looking and socially reactionary. It greatly enhanced provision and practice in science, design and technology and ICT, while censoring elements of other subjects which might develop socially critical understanding. History was not only Eurocentric, it was overwhelmingly about the development of the British state. There was to be no study of events within the past quarter century and no study of contemporary society or politics. Media Studies, surely a core element in any socially relevant curriculum, merited a brief mention within English. An official canon of texts was prescribed for English Literature. Finally, the prescription was reinforced by national tests at ages seven, eleven and fourteen, ensuring a degree of panic which would deter teachers from taking the risk of including non-prescribed learning. Unfortunately, most of the school improvement literature simply took this situation as given, and the present government's adviser Michael Barber went so far as to call the National Curriculum one of the 'four pillars of accountability'!

Little has been done to change this state of affairs and in some respects things have got worse. Primary teachers in England and Wales are compelled to teach a Literacy Hour each day, according to a national definition of content for each school term, and are obliged to emphasise grammatical terminology, which can distract from reading for enjoyment and searching for meaning. It is a more economical approach than the traditional primary practice of listening to each pupil read aloud each day but it denies teachers the professional discretion of judging when it is appropriate to consolidate and when to move forward. It also tends to divorce reading and writing from meaningful context linked to other subjects and it reduces the importance of oracy.

Despite such constraints, the teachers in the case study schools have had the courage and professional commitment to adapt the curriculum in ways that are in the best interests of their pupils.

Structured play has an important role in the early years but this has also been squeezed by innovations such as the Literacy Hour. Play of this kind fosters practice in everyday English in simulated contexts that relate to children's lives, such as the hospital or travel agents, builds creativity and confidence and enables the young child to try out new roles. All the case study primary schools incorporated structured play into their curriculum.

The *Literacy Hour* is either adapted by the schools to meet the needs of bilingual pupils or rejected in favour of better models. Either way, the links between written language, spoken language and experience are strengthened. The stress on teaching the metalanguage of textual structures is being converted into an equally explicit but more creative teaching of genres. The whole-class and group situations provide a new basis for developing confidence and motivation.

The creative and performing arts (Art, Dance, Drama, Literature, Media Studies and Music) have a particular prominence, within and beyond timetabled lessons. Although not well served by an official agenda which emphasises vocational utility and measurable skills in the curriculum, the arts are central to school improvement. They help pupils to concentrate and reflect, and to develop confidence, autonomy and co-operation. They lead to outcomes which do not depend upon written English and which are highly visible and publicly valued, including by their peers. They provide an important site for pupils to explore identities and the customs and values of the diverse cultures between which their lives move.

In many of the schools, opportunities are being sought in the *humanities* and in *English* to develop an appreciation of the achievements of different peoples and cultures, and an understanding of some of the tensions and conflicts in the modern world, such as the impact of poverty, racism and war, and the struggles against them.

In the secondary schools, *Asian languages* such as Bengali, Gujerati and Urdu are accorded comparable status to the traditionally taught Western European languages. They are seen both as 'community languages' – a means of maintaining contact with extended families – and as the bearers of a rich cultural heritage. In the primary schools, though less formally, pupils' home languages are encouraged, supported and valued, and bilingualism is regarded as an important achievement. This issue is also closely aligned with pupils' self-esteem.

The entitlement of bilingual pupils to *Information and Communication Technology*, despite the adverse conditions of some school buildings, is part of a commitment to equal opportunities, especially since many pupils do not have access to computers at home. In some schools the value of computers as a social technology, encouraging cooperation in school and new links with the wider world, is a motive for curriculum development.

Vocational courses such as Health and Social Care, Business Studies and Leisure and Tourism, as well as enhancing employment prospects, are also being used to develop communication and other skills in the urban environment, and greater independence and confidence in the adult and largely white-dominated world of business and officialdom.

Other initiatives in individual schools and education authorities have also been introduced with an eye to the needs of bilingual pupils for language development and a rich experience. These range from the integrated Foundation course in the first year of secondary, at Falinge Park, to the many curriculum enrichment opportunities in Birmingham schools. Extra-curricular activities are a strength in many schools and, by winning parents' trust, schools are involving Asian pupils in theatre performances and residential visits.

The *Eurocentricity* of the official curriculum is being challenged in many different respects, whilst guaranteeing pupils' right of access to the cultural capital of British and Western European tradition. Bilingual pupils are learning to value both Shakespeare's plays and Asian dance. The connections between school learning and the rest of life are being re-established, by linking to pupils' direct experiences of life in British cities and their grandparents' villages in Bangladesh. Secondary students are increasingly involved in community projects and campaigns, developing an active sense of citizenship in the overlapping spheres of ethnic community, city, nation state and world. This social engagement is linked to a critical understanding of power, based on class, gender and race; in some schools in particular, students are learning to challenge injustice and racism with confidence.

The themes linking these initiatives are several but interconnected:

- enhancing intercultural understanding
- encouraging active critical engagement
- fostering social responsibility
- accelerating linguistic and cognitive development.

They connect with particular strengths in teaching and learning which are characteristic of these schools.

Teaching and learning

In the introductory chapters, I referred to the theoretical perspectives of Vygotsky (1962, 1978), Driver (1983) and Edwards and Mercer (1987) – three interrelated developments of *social constructivism*. The various practices I saw on the ground provided fascinating illustrations within the context of educating bilingual pupils.

Social constructivism provides a basic pedagogical theory that leads to *powerful learning*. It is learner-centred in the sense that learners must construct their own meanings and models of reality, but it also has high expectations of the teacher. It places a premium on early assessment, not simply in terms of 'levels' but also in terms of bringing out into the open the learners' prior experiences and ways of seeing things. It demands the planning of activities and situations where the learners can confront experiences and do the thinking themselves. Finally, it requires precise interventions, so that misconceptions are challenged and new models clearly and explicitly presented at a deeply theoretical level.

The particular situation of bilingual pupils requires special skills within this general frame. They often have limited experience of the kinds of learning which schools traditionally value or of the choice of content favoured in the standard curriculum. They may be fluent in basic interpersonal and transaction English but have rarely heard or read the cognitively more demanding discourses used for discussing environmental or social issues in English. The extent to which they have done so in another language may also be extremely limited.

For these reasons, the development of *collaborative learning* which is *language-rich* and *cognition-focused* is particularly crucial. It requires careful planning and careful initiation of pupils into new ways of working but it greatly enhances cognitive development and fluency in a wide variety of discourses. Collaborative learning involves a reflective confrontation with new information and experiences and avoids the shallower 'replication' learning that results from didactic or transmission teaching.

Social constructivist perspectives are particularly important in light of the huge gulf that can exist between the life experience of the pupil and the teacher, the minority and the majority communities. Because bilingual learners' prior experience is marginalised by the selection of knowledge which is favoured in schools as the traditional or official curriculum, it is vital that teachers deploy strategies which bring that outside experience into the open. We need to help bilingual learners to find a voice.

There are many accounts in this book of such exciting learning activities, which enable bilingual pupils to explore and articulate their real-world experiences and make sense of the frequent intercultural shifts their lives demand. Bilingual learners need time to explore the differences between religious creeds and personal beliefs, traditional customs and peer-group expectations. They particularly need to be enabled to critique media representations of their lives and communities, and the blatant and subtle racism in texts of many genres. For reading of this nature, *critical literacy* (of a kind which is quite marginalised by the official literacy strategies) goes hand in hand with the negotiation of identities and cultures.

We customarily call speakers of other languages in our schools 'bilingual', but they are not so in a complete or ready-made sense. Most are emergent bilinguals or multilinguals whose use of all their languages needs support and development. Their needs differ greatly, and the expertise of EAL teachers and other bilingual staff, sometimes in close collaboration with learning support teachers, is needed to assess their linguistic and cognitive profiles. Some will have a clear scientific understanding but lack the English terminology. Some will be more comfortable discussing a hypothesis first in their mother tongue before contributing to the whole-class discussion in English. The encouragement of Asian languages is important not only in terms of self-respect and respect for family and community but also as a source of enrichment for the English language, which has always mined its riches from many sources.

The theories of 'multiple intelligences' are valuable in support of the arts, and can be applied to learning in a wide range of subjects. Learning is strengthened by the opening of visual, physical and musical channels. Encouraging the use of all the senses facilitates a wider range of expression of thoughts and feelings than writing alone. This has a special relevance for pupils who are not yet comfortable about expressing themselves in written English; other media cannot be a substitute but they build confidence which also accelerates the development of cognition and literacy.

Finally, this book has described many fine examples of teaching which lift the glass ceiling of achievement for bilingual pupils. While policy makers need to understand that many bilingual learners take longer to acquire particular skills to a testable level, they need also to recognise a duty of developing special talents, whether in mathematics or music. Often, co-operative learning which is well supported by exposure to classic texts will place achievements within the grasp of bilingual learners which individually would be unattainable, such as the poetry writing on *Macbeth* at Sparrow Hill Community School.

Ethos, motivation and maturity

There is frequent emphasis on good behaviour in the guidance for school improvement but this can be be achieved in different ways, some of which do little to promote pupil motivation. Struggling schools need to learn from those which have developed high levels of motivation and a true pride in learning. Pupils have a right to a harmonious environment where their learning is free from disruption, and Asian parents are the first to expect this. Recognised and acceptable sanctions have a part to play but should be based on the principled agreement of the whole school community. Many of the schools have involved pupils in drawing up behaviour policies and codes of practice which promote self-discipline and personal responsibility, and whose tone is inclusive rather than punitive. The school's aims are also owned by the whole community.

A key word is *respect*. This is resonant in meaning, with associations with Black consciousness and resistance. Respect signifies mutuality and justice. Teachers earn respect, and show respect to their pupils. It requires that any bullying or manifestation of racism will be challenged.

Pride in learning is characterised by commitment, enthusiasm, concentration, independence, co-operation and mutual respect. The expectation that pupils' work is not done merely as exercises for the teacher to correct, but will be shared with their peers, helps to promote these qualities even better than systems of extrinsic rewards.

In school after school, the quality of display not only celebrates achievement but improves the school ethos by enhancing self-esteem. The use of photographs of pupils and their activities, as well as the extensive involvement of pupils in presenting assemblies, are key features.

In many cases, the pupils' work has an audience and an effect beyond the school gates. The schools are involved in community projects, art is displayed to parents and in public places, and pupils are making a direct contribution to the well-being of the community through community placements and political campaigns. Those efforts and interests which are not initiated by the school, whether reading at mosque or helping a neighbour, are also celebrated within the school.

Mature responsibility is also promoted within the school as pupils take on adult roles in school councils, as play leaders and peer mediators, or in teaching their greater ICT skills to their own parents and teachers. Meeting mature young people who have been empowered by the leadership roles they have assumed has made a lasting impression on me.

When a positive ethos and respect for teachers pervades a school, negative attitudes in pupils are deterred by pressure from their peer group, and by the vigilance of staff who simply don't let the children reach a stage where they give up on themselves. Persistence on issues of attendance and disaffection, often extending to working with other influential adults in the child's life, pays good dividends. Pupils are supported by mentoring arrangements and by teachers who are so determined they will succeed that they are prepared to give extra help after school. In successful schools, all teachers understand that they have a serious pastoral role, and dedicated pastoral staff know they must also provide academic guidance and promote pupils' achievement. Circle time in primary schools, residentials and extracurricular activities, help to cement relationships and generate a positive sense of belonging.

The transition to secondary school is a particularly difficult time, and secondary schools in Scotland have repeatedly been criticised by the inspectorate for exposing the first two year-groups to too many different teachers (often twenty or more!) It was particularly interesting to learn of the success of the 'Foundation' programme at Falinge Park – aided by good teamwork and the sharing of expertise, pupils' progress significantly increased when they were taught by only a few teachers.

The ethos of achievement also extends to staff and parents, as pupils are shown the diverse talents of their teachers and see their parents attending school-based community courses and receiving awards.

Inner city schools operate within a troubled social environment in which all sorts of contradictory behaviours and values are displayed. Some of these are extremely negative, as poverty and despair result in the oppressed turning on those who are not to blame. Schools have to create an extremely powerful counter-culture to the macho street culture outside. This is only possible when a warm and positive ethos and community is built within the school and when the school's values link across to the positive traditions of working-class and minority communities.

The wider community

Only one of the schools in this book is designated and funded as a community school, yet most of them have assumed this function to a significant degree. There are many models of 'community school', including some which only amount to providing a few classrooms for some adult education classes during the evening. In others, there is a philosophy and practice of community development and lifelong learning which in turn impacts on the quality of learning of school-age pupils. This is what these schools are concerned with.

The key role of community and parental liaison is being strongly developed in many of the schools featured here, and the resourceful individuals who undertake it are piloting new practices as they go. Their duties may include interpreting and translating, home visits, supporting pastoral staff and welfare officers, and liaising with new parents. They act as ambassadors for the school and explain the school's structure and curriculum to parents unfamiliar with it. They are involved in parents' evenings and community events. They help to overcome parental fears and develop trust and cooperation. They help to increase parental involvement in children's learning. Their expertise is grounded in their intercultural understanding and experience and their commitment to the local community, of which they are often well-known members. Individual teachers, classroom assistants and the headteacher will frequently share this work with the staff member who is designated as community liaison worker.

Parents often fear becoming involved in schools and do not fully understand how they work. They may have had negative experiences of schools or officialdom themselves, or find the school's approach to education quite different from their own experience of schooling. Their absence from parents' evenings, for example, should never be mistaken for indifference towards their children's education. Some primary schools have found ways of involving even parents who cannot read in their first languages in listening to their children read at home. Parents distrustful of the arts or fearful of losing control of their daughters have learnt to take pride in their children's achievements and to grasp the new opportunities offered to their children of university and career. An untapped resource exists in older brothers and sisters, and schools would do well to focus more attention on guiding these willing mentors and home-tutors.

Adult education in community schools can have a powerful influence in many directions. It can develop the English language and literacy of parents of young children, to their own and their children's benefit. Parenting courses provide an understanding of the educational value of play and the possibilities for early conceptual development. The location of such adult education within the school makes more parents feel secure enough to participate, and links closely with classroom-based involvement. In some communities, the school provides mothers with a crucial escape from isolation and a unique opportunity for their own personal and career development. Community learners are increasingly keen on formal accreditation, and their children are greatly encouraged by seeing learning so valued by adults. Community schools can also increase the supply of bilingual staff for the school and so improve the opportunities for parents and teachers to develop new understandings of community issues and education.

Schools rarely draw extensively on the geographical and social knowledge of the local community, hardly ever invite adults from it into school to speak to pupils, make little direct use of the diverse cultural interests of parents. Extended visits overseas are a serious problem for many pupils but, when they are unavoidable, schools have not exploited the potential opportunities for extending pupils' learning. There are some valuable exceptions, but we could go further in this direction towards building a community curriculum.

Lessons for policy makers

The present government clearly shows concern to raise achievement but is making many contradictions in its policy. The core strategy of 'combining pressure and support' is leading to uneasy shifts between carrot and stick.

League tables continue to deter many young teachers from working in inner-city schools, fearing that their careers will be blighted by relatively low examination results. Moreover, the tables encourage many concerned parents to look elsewhere for school places. Rigid or inappropriate expectations which don't reflect the progress of the children who entered school with limited English tend to demoralise many schools.

Performance-related pay for teachers is likely to exacerbate such damage. It will benefit teachers in more affluent areas, where they can show higher attainment with less effort, rather than the dedicated staff who work exceedingly hard in disadvantaged areas. It will undoubtedly turn teacher against teacher, and undermine the teamwork upon which these schools depend. It is high time that the teachers working many additional hours to ensure the success of bilingual pupils are properly paid for their overtime.

Little account is taken in official statistics of late arrivers in schools. In schools with many vacant places, this can seriously distort value-added measures. When this includes pupils who have been expelled or 'encouraged to leave' other schools, or pupils newly arrived from overseas, there are particular challenges. None of this is adequately recognised or funded. The allocation of budgets to schools based entirely on a form completed in January fails to take account of late arrivers, whose education is only funded from much later on.

The quality of language development services has been progressively undermined by short-term funding for over a decade, and many expert teachers have chosen to take up mainstream posts in schools so as to escape career uncertainty. Now LEA services are being disbanded and funding transferred to schools, where it may be used in other ways. Schools which are seeking to hold on to EAL teachers by taking them onto their payrolls are finding even this difficult, as the devolved budgets prove inadequate and are guaranteed for only a two-year period.

The quality of language development teachers depends not only on their relationships with other colleagues in schools but also on staff development and exchange of ideas between EAL teachers within an LEA or region. In Rochdale, for example, longstanding arrangements concentrated non-teaching time onto a particular afternoon to facilitate joint training and resource development, whether by the EAL specialists or mainstream teachers whom they could release.

Such authority-wide training is now jeopardised by breaking up LEA services. EAL specialists who receive little staff development themselves are not well prepared to develop the expertise of mainstream colleagues. The current devolution also prevents the flexible deployment of expertise to schools receiving bilingual pupils for the first time or where particular linguistic knowledge is needed, and will make it far more difficult to respond to the needs of asylum seekers.

Both initial and in-service training for mainstream teachers in educating bilingual pupils are extremely limited. Some teacher education institutes in areas where there are many bilingual pupils lack either specialist or elective courses in bilingual education. The recruitment of bilingual teachers is woefully limited, despite excellent initiatives in a few universities and colleges.

The community education which many schools have developed goes unrecognised and unfunded, unless schools can negotiate their way through the uncertain channels of joining Education Action Zones or achieving special status. Courses in parenting, literacy and educational play, and the provision of dedicated book and toy libraries, are rare and uncertainly funded.

Because of settlement patterns, many Asian communities live in inner-city areas, and their school buildings are old and sometimes overcrowded. Funding to replace or expand them has been inadequate to the task, and schools are forced to delve into their own delegated budgets to provide a welcoming and stimulating learning environment. This structural inequality amounts to a special form of institutional racism in our public administration of educational resources.

Finally, the admirable practice described in this book and the philosophy of empowerment it expresses are undermined by bureaucratic models of school development focusing on top-down control.

Antiracism today and tomorrow

For many years, it has been accepted that some types of 'multicultural' education are superficial and tokenistic. Simply inserting the tokens of 'samosas, saris and steel drums' into the curriculum and school events is only a starting point. That's not to deny the value of such recognition of other cultures – indeed, this is a vital and symbolic way of showing we value pupils and communities – but it just isn't enough. In addition, a tokenistic multiculturalism tends to imply that culture is both decorative and frozen, and that bilingual youngsters live in a cultural environment which is rosy, singular and unproblematic.

This inadequacy has been challenged under the banner of 'anti-racism', but in the process there have been some serious efforts. Educators have to recognise the real pain experienced by victims of racism and the need to challenge racism institutions and oppression. However, some antiracist work has been disempowering. As Gus John and his colleagues have forcefully argued, an active opposition to racism cannot be achieved through filling white students or teachers with a sense of guilt.

> Since the assumption is that black students are the victims of the immoral behaviour of white students, white students almost inevitably become the 'baddies'. The operation of the antiracist policies almost inevitably results in white students (and their parents) feeling 'attacked' and all being seen as 'racist', whether they are ferret-eyed fascists or committed antiracists or simply children with a great store of human feeling and warmth who are ready to listen and learn and to explore their feelings towards one another... The notion that all white people are 'racist' is part of the racism awareness training (RAT) model... In practice, it has been an unmitigated disaster. It has re-inforced the guilt of many well-meaning whites and paralysed them when any issue of race arises... This simple model assumes that there is uniform access to power by all whites, and a uniform denial of access and power to all blacks. Clearly, this is not the case. We so not believe that an effective antiracist policy can exist unless the other issues are also addressed and dealt with, in particular class and gender. (see Macdonald, 1989, pp347-348).

Antiracist education in schools it not about creating higher levels of antagonism or negativity, but about developing the confidence, determination and knowledge of all students to challenge oppressive practices.

Teachers express their antiracist commitment in many ways. They work extremely hard to remove barriers to achievement and to encourage bilingual pupils to reach for the sky. They develop a school ethos characterised by good relationships and learning, one where any oppressive behaviour is out of place. However, depending on the age of the pupils, antiracism also entails the development of critical understanding and the exploration of new forms of citizenship education and community involvement. That is why the work in media education and the humanities, the campaigns around football and so on, are of such significance. These practices are still far too rare even in multi-ethnic schools.

Antiracism has emphasised key differences between oppression based on race and other forms of injustice and inequality. This doesn't mean that other aspects of equal opportunities can be ignored. A Pakistani girl growing up in Bradford may be affected by poor housing and her elder brothers' unemployment and depressed by patriarchal relationships within her own family. She needs the intellectual and personal resources to overcome all these problems. Patriarchal expectations are ultimately limiting of both boys and girls, and, if they are to prosper, bilingual youngsters have to work out how to position themselves not only within the Asian community but within a wider working community.

I emphasised at the start of this book the importance of a broad definition of learning and achievement. Education is not simply about measurable attainment but also about a wide spectrum of intellectual, moral and cultural achievement. Unless we extend our vision to include social understanding and empowerment, even the highest attaining bilingual students will find themselves stranded amidst the unjust structures and traditions of our society, and the individual success of a few will do nothing to improve the lives of the wider community.

Appendix

A brief guide for overseas readers

The majority of primary schools in **England** begin at age 5 and finish at 11. They may also include a nursery class.

Secondary schools in most areas begin at 11 and continue to age 16 or 18. In the former case, pupils may then proceed to a college. Education is compulsory to age 16. All the English secondary schools in this book are for 11-16 year olds. University normally begins at age 18. Most state-funded secondary schools are comprehensive, including all those in this book, although their real intake will vary according to their location and the pressures of parental choice and competition.

The years of formal education are designated by Years 1-11. These are grouped together as Key Stages. Primary schools contain Year 1-2 (Key Stage 1), and Years 3-6 (Key Stage 2). Classes for younger pupils are called Nursery and Reception. 11-16 year olds in secondary school are in Years 7-9 (Key Stage 3) and Years 10-11 (Key Stage 4). The content of the curriculum is largely determined by the National Curriculum, which now includes detailed prescription for Literacy and Numeracy Hours in primary schools.

At the end of Key Stages 1, 2 and 3, pupils sit national tests in English, Mathematics and Science (SATs), supplemented by teacher assessment. However, whatever their performance, it is not customary to repeat years except for serious medical reasons. At age sixteen, they sit the GCSE (General Certificate of Secondary Education), normally in about eight subjects. The higher grades are designated A*-C, the lower D-G.

The proportion of 16-year-old pupils in a school achieving five or more A*-C grades is an important official indicator of the school's overall attainment levels. (In 1999, approximately 48 per cent of pupils nationally reached this level.) Official statistics use the proportion of pupils entitled to free school meals as an indicator of socio-economic context, in order to 'benchmark' the performance of schools against those which are roughly similar. The proportion of pupils with EAL is not taken into account when comparing 'similar' schools.

In recent years, after the serious constraints of the early years of the National Curriculum, greater freedom has been given to study non-National Curriculum subjects such as Media Studies or pre-vocational courses such as Leisure and Tourism during Key Stage 4. Such courses are often accredited through the GNVQ rather than GCSE.

In primary school, each class is normally taught for all subjects by a single teacher. The classes are of mixed ability, although within them pupils may be grouped on different tables for English or mathematics so that appropriate work is set.

In secondary school, pupils are normally taught by a different teacher for each subject, as well as a form tutor (registration and pastoral). For particular subjects, pupils may be taught in 'sets' (classes doing work of differing levels of difficulty). Classes which are not so divided are called 'mixed-ability'. The practice of 'streaming' (i.e. dividing the population into different 'ability levels' across all their subjects) has largely been abandoned, because of its demoralising effect on the lower streams and because pupils' capabilities vary strongly between subjects.

As well as the standard National Curriculum subjects, pupils also have lessons in Personal and Social Education (PSE). In addition to subject teachers, most secondary schools have Special Needs or Learning Support teachers, who withdraw pupils from classes for extra help or support them within a mainstream lesson. Schools with large numbers of bilingual pupils have EAL (English as an additional language, also known as ESL) or Language Development teachers, with a similar work pattern.

Schools are administered and supported by a local education authority (LEA) for each urban or rural area. Schools have primary responsibility for their own quality assurance and development, though under the broad supervision of the LEA. They are inspected every six years, and sometimes more frequently, by OFSTED, a governmental agency. In some inner city areas, new developments intended to raise achievement are coordinated by an education action zone (EAZ), which has some freedom to experiment and additional funds.

* * *

The system of education in **Scotland** has many similarities to the English system but has developed separately. The following notes highlight significant differences, to the extent that this will help the reader. The Scottish schools featured in Part B are Dalry Primary School and Shawlands Academy.

In Scotland, pupils are usually twelve years old when they transfer to secondary school. The primary classes are called P1-P7. All state secondary schools run to age 18. The classes are called S1-S4 (the compulsory years) and S5-S6, which lead directly on to university. All state secondary schools are comprehensive, although, as in England, there is a social imbalance of intake in the large cities.

There is a less rigid curriculum, based on guidelines for ages 5-14. The curriculum for older pupils is based on examination syllabuses. Pupils sit Standard Grade at age 16, in seven to eight subjects. The grade boundaries do not correspond with the GCSE, and grades are grouped into Credit, General and Foundation. The proportion of pupils achieving five or more Credit grades (just under 30 per cent nationally) is one official marker of attainment in a school.

Instead of national tests for all children at a particular age, primary school teachers set English and Mathematics tests at an appropriate level of difficulty as and when pupils attain that level.

Each secondary school has a number of Guidance staff with a pastoral function, including teaching PSE. To some extent, this reduces the expectation that other teachers will concern themselves with pastoral issues affecting learning.

The Education Authority (EA) has greater control than in England. Schools have the prime responsibility for quality assurance, using a framework of performance indicators known as 'How Good is our School?' They are inspected by HMI (Her Majesty's Inspectors), though less frequently than in England.

There are many other significant differences but they should not affect the understanding of this book.

Bibliography

Blair, Maud *et al.* (1998) *Making the Difference: teaching and learning strategies in successful multi-ethnic schools.* London, DfEE/Open University.

Blasé, J and J R (1994) *Empowering Teachers – What Successful Principals Do.* Thousand Oaks CA., Corwin Press

Bowring-Carr, C and West-Burnham, J (1997) *Effective Learning in Schools: how to integrate learning and leadership for a successful school.* London, Pitman.

Cooke, S (1998) *Collaborative Learning Activities in the Classroom: designing inclusive materials for learning and language development.* Leicester, Resource Centre for Multicultural Education.

Cummins, J (1996) *Negotiating Identities.* Ontario, CA CABE

Driver, R (1983) *The Pupil as Scientist.* Milton Keynes, Open University.

Edwards, D and Mercer, N (1987) *Common Knowledge.* London, Methuen.

Fullan, M (1992) *Successful School Improvement.* (Introduction by M Huberman) Buckingham, Open University Press.

Fullan, M (1993) *Change Forces.* London, Falmer.

Gray, J *et al.* (1999) *Improving Schools.* Buckingham, Open University Press

Green, P *ed.* (for DIECEC) (1999) *Raise the Standard: a practical guide to raising ethnic minority and bilingual pupils' achievement.* Stoke on Trent, Trentham Books.

Joyce, B and Showers, B (1988) *Student Achievement through Staff Development.* London, Longman.

Joyce, B *et al.* (1997) *Models of Learning – tools for teaching.* London, Longman.

Joyce, B *et al.* (1999) *The New Structure of School Improvement: inquiring schools and achieving students.* Buckingham, Open University Press.

Leat, D (1998) *Thinking through Geography.* Cambridge, Chris Kingston Publishing.

MacBeath, J *ed* (1998) *Effective School Leadership: responding to change.* London, Paul Chapman.

Macdonald, I *et al.* (1989) *Murder in the Playground. The Report of the Macdonald Inquiry into racism and racial violence in Manchester schools.* London, Longsight Press.

National Commission on Education (1996) *Learning to Succeed*. London, Routledge.

OFSTED (1997) *From Failure to Success: how special measures are helping schools improve*. London, OFSTED.

OFSTED (1995) *Guidance on the Inspection of Secondary Schools*. London, HMSO.

Rose, S (1998) *Lifelines: biology, freedom, determinism*. London, Penguin.

Rudduck, J (1991) *Innovation and Change*. Milton Keynes, Open University Press

Scottish Office (1996) *How Good is our School?: self-evaluation using performance indicators*. Edinburgh, Scottish Office.

Stoll, L and Fink, D (1995) *Changing our Schools*. Buckingham, Open University Press

Stoll, L and Myers, K (1998) *No Quick Fixes: perspectives on schools in difficulty*. London, Falmer.

Vernon, L (1999) *How to Maximise the Benefits and Minimise the Adverse Effects of Pupils' Extended Visits Overseas*. Leicester, MELAS.

Vygotsky, L S (1962) *Thought and Language*. Cambridge Mass., MIT Press

Vygotsky, L S (1978) *Mind in Society*. London, Harvard University Press

Wrigley, T (1997) Raising Achievement for Asian Pupils. *Multicultural Teaching* 16/1

Wrigley, T (2000) Misunderstanding School Improvement. *Improving Schools* 3/1

Index

Bold type indicates the first page of a section on this topic